Walt and Winn

Wondrous Words

Level One

An important handbook to help parents, teachers and students of the English language really widen vocabulary in a fun way

Copyright © 2011 by Charlie Chaleco. 301861-CHAL
Library of Congress Control Number   2011912957
ISBN: Softcover   978-1-4653-0227-4
        Hardcover   978-1-4653-0228-1

All rights reserved. No part of this book may
be reproduced or transmitted in any form or by
any means, electronic or mechanical, including
photocopying, recording, or by any information
storage and retrieval system, without permission in
writing from the copyright owner.

This book was printed in the United States of
America.

To order additional copies of this book, contact:
Xlibris Corporation
0-800-644-6988
www.xlibrispublishing.co.uk
Orders@Xlibrispublishing.co.uk

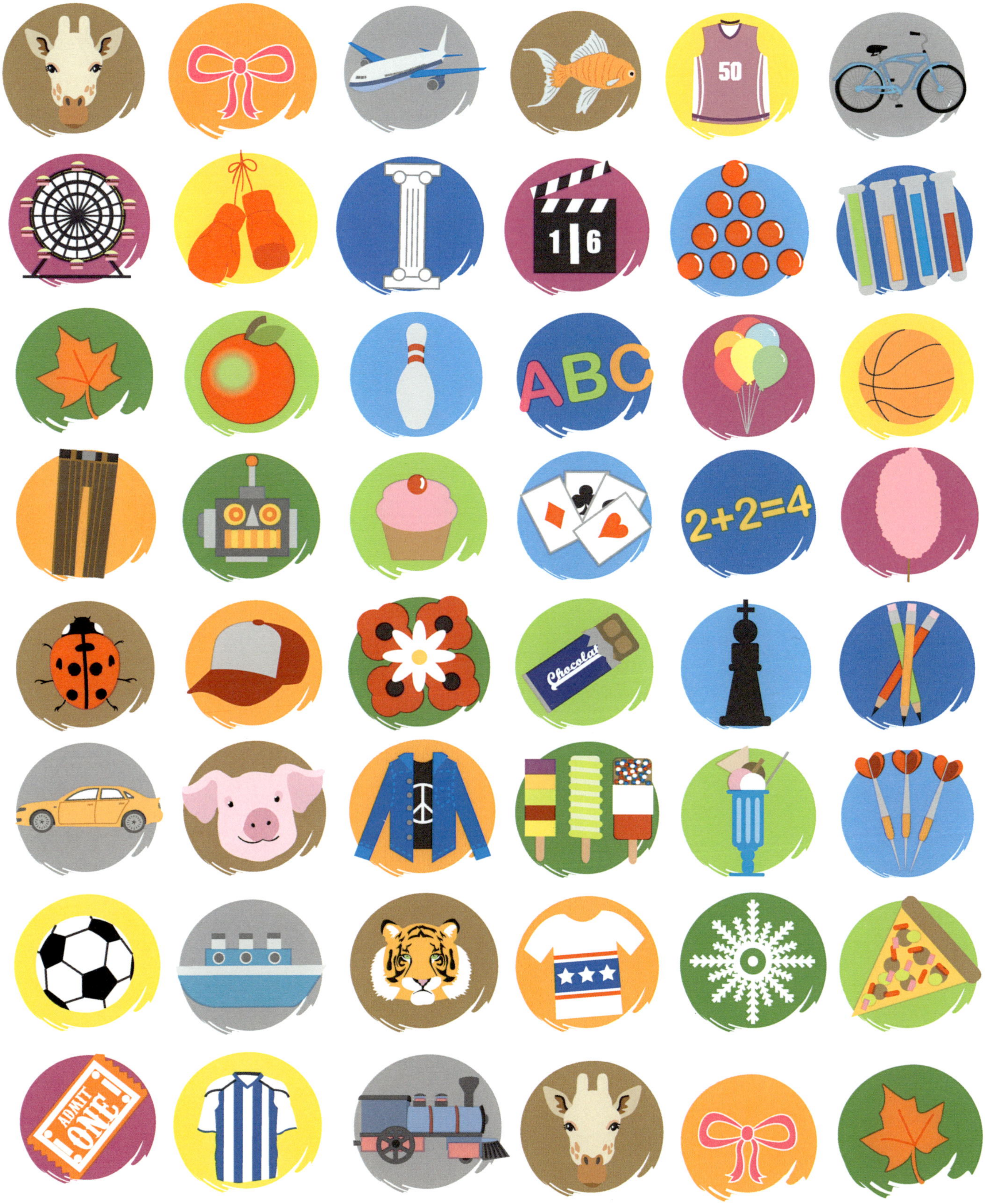
50
1 6
ABC
2+2=4
Chocolat
ADMIT ONE!

This book is dedicated to
my mother, Anne.
Many thanks for all the help and advice from my lovely wife Dolors, my daughter Martina, my good friend Paul, friends Nigel and Julie and students Ethan, Daniel and Caroline who have been very receptive guinea pigs

Charlie Chaleco

Copyright and legal

All rights reserved. In all countries, no part of this publication may be resold, reproduced or transmitted in any form or by any means, or stored in a retrieval system of any nature without prior written permission (except the photocopiable pages)from the copyright holder of the publisher´s address.
Application for permission for use of copyright material shall be made to the publisher. Full acknowledgement of author, publisher and source must be given.
The Primary Language Consultants is the sole proprieter of the name "Walt and Winnie´s Wondrous Words, the name "Charlie Chaleco", the comic story, crosswords and word searches. The use of these in any form being strictly prohibited unless formally authorised by contract with The Primary Language Consultants.

Welcome to
Walt and Winnie's
Wondrous Words

Statistics show that children have a vocabulary only half the size as fifty years ago. This impoverishment must be addressed! After teaching for many years, I realised that there appeared to be a great lack of resources to enable teachers to introduce our children to the Wondrous Words of the English language. Furthermore, two things happened that sparked me into action:

Firstly, Caroline, a student of mine, complained that when she looked in the dictionary to find the meaning of a word, in the definition she found three more words she didn´t understand!

Secondly, I questioned my friend's use of the word 'facetious'. Brian thought it meant "a nasty, cutting remark", whilst I explained it actually means "amusing, frivolous remarks when things should be taken more seriously".
These incidents confirmed it was time to create a fun user-friendly guide to the English Language, and so 'Wondrous Words' was born.

Charlie Chaleco

Written and Art directed by
Charlie Chaleco
Designed and Illustrated by
The Hidden Dingbat Collective

Contents

Section 1..................................p. 13

Section 2..................................p. 21

Section 3..................................p. 29

Section 4..................................p. 37

Section 5..................................p. 45

Section 6..................................p. 53

Section 7..................................p. 61

Section 8..................................p. 69

Section 9..................................p. 77

Section 10................................p. 85

Walt Wosencroft

Winnie Wilson

Walt and Winnie are great friends. They're going for a summer break to Walt's gran's place in the country

They arrive at the old house and would you believe it, it's raining!

Walt: Well as it's raining so heavily, let's go and explore this place
Winnie : Good idea!

Winnie: we'll start at the very top – the attic.

Walt: It's so dark and dusty here!

Winnie: There's so much stuff up here, like this old trunk.

Walt: I wonder what's inside?

Winnie: No treasure! Just some dirty old books!

Walt: Wondrous Words by Waltrina Wosencroft

Walt: She must be one of my ancestors!

Winnie: What tiny, handwritten words!

Winnie reading from book: "Prattle – to talk in a foolish way"

Walt: All these words!

Walt: "An oaf – a clumsy, stupid person" Ha, ha, ha!

Walt: Let´s go and show gran.

Winnie: We found this in the attic. Looks like it was written by someone in your family.

Gran: Oh yes! I remember Aunty Waltrina when I was a girl.

Gran: She used to be a schoolmistress in the local school.

Gran: She used to take her job very seriously. And she loved teaching new words.

Gran: She would read the meanings from the class dictionary

Gran: … and write them in books like that one.

Gran: She would spend hours writing so neatly!

Walt: Look at the rain streaming down the windows! No cycling in the country!

Winnie: I think we should do something with those "Wondrous Words."

Winnie: We could completely modernise the book on our laptops!

Walt: And we can create some word games to go with them.

Walt and Winnie get to work.

Walt and Winnie: And look what we´ve made!

9

Winnie: We've printed it out with lots of colour pictures.

Walt: It's now easy to read and with crosswords, wordsearches and other games

Walt: We thought about the layout. We've split the book into ten sections of fifty words.

The Wondrous Words Game goes like this ………

Winnie: It means "juicy" and begins with the letter L?

Walt: And the other person has to say the word. **Luscious.** Then you change over.

Gran: Aunty Waltrina would have been so pleased with what you've done. I'm surprised she never did anything with those books.

Winnie: She probably met some hunk, got married and had lots of children! No time for books then!

The Wondrous Words Game

After each section of 50 words you can test your understanding by having a go at the **crosswords** and the **word searches**.

You can also play the **Wondrous Words Game** with a partner. To do this you can find the WW Question cards in the website or simply choose any 5 words for each person from a section.

Player 1 says the meaning of a word and the first letter. If **Player 2** answers with the correct word he or she scores 10 points.

For example:

Player 1: A book of maps beginning with an "A"?
Player 2: "Easy, it´s an atlas!"

Player 1 says 4 more meanings and the first letters and you total up the points.

Then it´s **Player 2** who says 5 meanings and the first letter and you see who the winner is.

You can make it a bit trickier by awarding another 10 points for the correct spellings.

When you are getting all the words in that section fixed into permanent memory you can move on the next section.

Phonetical Code

Usually English words stress the first part (syllable). If this is not the case, or some further clarification is necessary, I have put the stressed syllable in capital letters.

eg. *bi WIL derd*.

Use the phonetical code below to pronounce the words correctly.

a as **cat**
ay as in **say**
air as in **pair**
ar as in **hard**
c as in **cat**
ee as in **feed**
eer as in **deer**
ei as in **mile**
er as in **girl**
i as in **bit**
y as in **sky** (with no vowel in front)
y as in **you** (at the beginning of a word)
j as in **jump**
cw as in **quick**
oh as in **goes**
oi as in **noise**
oo as in **soon**
ow as in **cow**
s as in **yes**
uh as in **fighter**
z as in **buys**
zh as in **erasure**

Wondrous Words

Section One

WALTRINA WOSENCROFT

"I find it absolutely absurd how some children pronounce the consonant aitch incorrectly."

Absurd
(ub SERD or ub ZERD)
senseless

Achieve
(uh CHEEV)
to succeed in doing or getting

Aitch
(aych)
the letter h

Castigate
to punish

Conduct
behaviour

Consonant
any letter which is not a vowel

Convenient
(con VEE ni unt)
suitable, at hand

Courteous
(CER ti us)
well mannered, showing respect to others

Definition
(def in ISH un)
the meaning of a word

Destination
(des tin AY shun)
the place you are heading for

Encourage
(en CUH rij)
to give support, to spur on

Erase
(i RAYZ)
to rub out

Essential
(es EN shul)
something vital

Evaporate
(i VAP uh rayt)
to disappear; when a liquid turns to gas

Exaggerate
(eg ZAJ uh rayt)
to make a greater number or amount than there really is

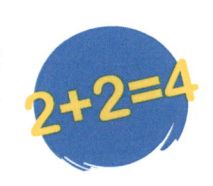

Execution
(ex ic YOO shun)
the putting to death as a punishment

Forbid
(fuh BID)
to refuse to allow

Instantaneous
(in stun TAY ni us)
straight away

Imbecile
an idiot

Infuriating
(inf YOR ri ayt ing)
something that makes you really angry

"I bet your great aunty was really strict. She'd say, "I forbid this incessant chatter! I find it most infuriating."

15

"She'd say to you, "One thing is to be a jovial boy. Another is to be a ludicrous oaf!""

Jovial
(JOH vi ul)
good-humoured, joking, funny

Lenient
(LEEN i unt)
not strict

Livid
very angry

Ludicrous
(LOO di crus)
ridiculous, silly

Mediocre
(mee di OH cuh)
only average

Mimic
to copy

Monotonous
(muh NOT uh nus)
lacking variety, boring

Nicotine
(NIC uh teen)
the main drug in tobacco that gets you addicted

Notion
(NOH shun)
an idea

Oaf
a clumsy, stupid person

Occasionally
(uc AY zhun uli)
sometimes

Parentheses
(pa REN thuh seez)
brackets in writing

Penultimate
(pen UL tim ut)
the one next to the last

Percussion
(puh CUSH un)
a musical instrument, like a drum

Prattle
to talk in a foolish way, to chatter

Prologue
the introduction at the beginning of a story

Punctual
arriving or happening at the exact agreed time

Quarrel
(CWO rul)
to argue; an argument

Quill
(CWIL)
a large feather used as a pen in olden times

Rebuke
(rib YOOC)
to reprimand, to tell off

"Occasionally, she would rebuke the pupils for not being punctual."

"If you gave the incorrect response to a question about synonyms or syllables she'd lower her spectacles and say, "I will not tolerate this slipshod comportment.""

Reprimand
to get a good telling off

Response
(ri SPONS)
an answer

Soluble
(SOL yuh bl)
can be dissolved

Spectacles
glasses

Syllable
(SIL ubl)
one part of a word

Synonym
(SIN uh nim)
a word having the same meaning

Task
a job to be done

Tolerate
to allow; to put up with different views

Tardy
arriving late

Wrath
(ROTH)
great anger

Crossword

Across:

1. The letter h
3. A clumsy, stupid person
6. An idea
7. Very angry
8. A job to do
12. Great Anger
13. It´s really needed

Down:

1. To get what you´re after
2. There are 21 in the alphabet
4. Really crazy
5. Will not allow
9. To rub out
10. To copy
11. An old-fashioned pen

Word Search

```
E R T E R E T O R T M N B T M
N H T Y J I I T A M O P P Q E
C A S T I G A T E T I T P M D
O T Q N I C O T I N E Y E O I
U R E C O N D U C T O I R O O
R D F H I K L P O T O M C M C
A B Y W E R Y T U M P B U T R
G I E X A G G E R A T E S P E
E A L I B O N G A O I C S R A
L A U R O G G Y G Q R I I A N
E V A P O R A T E T T L O T N
O U R R B R A L E N I E N T E
T T O R R I D R A N I L O L Q
W T A T U N Q U A R R E L E T
C A B O M O N O T O N O U S O
```

School
1. Castigate
2. Conduct
3. Encourage
4. Evaporate
5. Exaggerate
6. Imbecile
7. Lenient
8. Mediocre
9. Nicotine
10. Monotonous
11. Percussion
12. Prattle
13. Quarrel
14. Retort
15. Torrid

This page is photocopiable for classroom use only.

19

SECTION 1 - CHECKLIST

1. Absurd
- ☐ Understood
- ☐ Used in speech
- ☐ Used in writing

2. Achieve
- ☐ Understood
- ☐ Used in speech
- ☐ Used in writing

3. Aitch
- ☐ Understood
- ☐ Used in speech
- ☐ Used in writing

4. Castigate
- ☐ Understood
- ☐ Used in speech
- ☐ Used in writing

5. Conduct
- ☐ Understood
- ☐ Used in speech
- ☐ Used in writing

6. Consonant
- ☐ Understood
- ☐ Used in speech
- ☐ Used in writing

7. Convenient
- ☐ Understood
- ☐ Used in speech
- ☐ Used in writing

8. Courteous
- ☐ Understood
- ☐ Used in speech
- ☐ Used in writing

9. Definition
- ☐ Understood
- ☐ Used in speech
- ☐ Used in writing

10. Destination
- ☐ Understood
- ☐ Used in speech
- ☐ Used in writing

11. Encourage
- ☐ Understood
- ☐ Used in speech
- ☐ Used in writing

12. Erase
- ☐ Understood
- ☐ Used in speech
- ☐ Used in writing

13. Essential
- ☐ Understood
- ☐ Used in speech
- ☐ Used in writing

14. Evaporate
- ☐ Understood
- ☐ Used in speech
- ☐ Used in writing

15. Exaggerate
- ☐ Understood
- ☐ Used in speech
- ☐ Used in writing

16. Execution
- ☐ Understood
- ☐ Used in speech
- ☐ Used in writing

17. Forbid
- ☐ Understood
- ☐ Used in speech
- ☐ Used in writing

18. Instantaneous
- ☐ Understood
- ☐ Used in speech
- ☐ Used in writing

19. Imbecile
- ☐ Understood
- ☐ Used in speech
- ☐ Used in writing

20. Infuriating
- ☐ Understood
- ☐ Used in speech
- ☐ Used in writing

21. Jovial
- ☐ Understood
- ☐ Used in speech
- ☐ Used in writing

22. Lenient
- ☐ Understood
- ☐ Used in speech
- ☐ Used in writing

23. Livid
- ☐ Understood
- ☐ Used in speech
- ☐ Used in writing

24. Ludicrous
- ☐ Understood
- ☐ Used in speech
- ☐ Used in writing

25. Mediocre
- ☐ Understood
- ☐ Used in speech
- ☐ Used in writing

26. Mimic
- ☐ Understood
- ☐ Used in speech
- ☐ Used in writing

27. Monotonous
- ☐ Understood
- ☐ Used in speech
- ☐ Used in writing

28. Nicotine
- ☐ Understood
- ☐ Used in speech
- ☐ Used in writing

29. Notion
- ☐ Understood
- ☐ Used in speech
- ☐ Used in writing

30. Oaf
- ☐ Understood
- ☐ Used in speech
- ☐ Used in writing

31. Occasionally
- ☐ Understood
- ☐ Used in speech
- ☐ Used in writing

32. Parentheses
- ☐ Understood
- ☐ Used in speech
- ☐ Used in writing

33. Penultimate
- ☐ Understood
- ☐ Used in speech
- ☐ Used in writing

34. Percussion
- ☐ Understood
- ☐ Used in speech
- ☐ Used in writing

35. Prattle
- ☐ Understood
- ☐ Used in speech
- ☐ Used in writing

36. Prologue
- ☐ Understood
- ☐ Used in speech
- ☐ Used in writing

37. Punctual
- ☐ Understood
- ☐ Used in speech
- ☐ Used in writing

38. Quarrel
- ☐ Understood
- ☐ Used in speech
- ☐ Used in writing

39. Quill
- ☐ Understood
- ☐ Used in speech
- ☐ Used in writing

40. Rebuke
- ☐ Understood
- ☐ Used in speech
- ☐ Used in writing

41. Reprimand
- ☐ Understood
- ☐ Used in speech
- ☐ Used in writing

42. Response
- ☐ Understood
- ☐ Used in speech
- ☐ Used in writing

43. Soluble
- ☐ Understood
- ☐ Used in speech
- ☐ Used in writing

44. Spectacles
- ☐ Understood
- ☐ Used in speech
- ☐ Used in writing

45. Syllable
- ☐ Understood
- ☐ Used in speech
- ☐ Used in writing

46. Synonym
- ☐ Understood
- ☐ Used in speech
- ☐ Used in writing

47. Task
- ☐ Understood
- ☐ Used in speech
- ☐ Used in writing

48. Tolerate
- ☐ Understood
- ☐ Used in speech
- ☐ Used in writing

49. Tardy
- ☐ Understood
- ☐ Used in speech
- ☐ Used in writing

50. Wrath
- ☐ Understood
- ☐ Used in speech
- ☐ Used in writing

Wondrous Words

Section Two

"Walt, don´t devour that caramel bar! It has to be consumed slowly."

Artery
a tube that carries blood from the heart

Available
(uh VAYL uh bl)
ready for use

Agriculture
farming

Astonished
(uh STON isht)
surprised

Bleak
dark, grim

Consumed
(cons YOOMD)
eaten or drunk

Caramel
a toffee

Dominate
to control with power

Devour
(div OW uh)
to eat greedily

Dejected
(di JEC tud)
depressed

Disapprove
(dis up ROOV)
to have a bad opinion of something

Eradicate
(i RAD i cayt)
to destroy, to get rid of

Edible
eatable

Exceedingly
(ec SEED ing li)
extremely

Enclose
(en CLOHZ)
to surround

Falter
(FOL tuh)
to hesitate

Garnished
decorated

Glutton
a greedy pig!

Grotesque
(gro TESC)
hideous

Haul
(horl)
to pull

"This **exceedingly** large cake is **garnished** with **edible** flowers."

"I have **indigestion**. I found the Italian food **irresistible** but now my **intestines** are blocked up!"

Heave
to pull upwards

Hesitate
(HEZ i tayt)
to hold back from doing something because of doubt

Indigestion
(in di JEST yun)
stomach ache

Indulge
(in DULJ)
to take part in something with great enthusiasm

Ingredient
(in GREE di unt)
something that is a part of a mixture

Intestines
(in TEST eenz) long tubes where you digest food

Irresistible
(iri ZIST ubl)
very tempting; impossible to turn down

Lavatory
(LAV uh tri)
a toilet

Luscious
(LUSH us)
juicy

Maniac
(MAY ni ac)
a mad person

Marquee
(mar CEE)
a large outdoor tent used at a party or an exhibition

Morsels
small pieces of food

Nourishment
(NUH rish munt)
food

Occur
(uh CER)
to happen

Poultry
(POHL tri)
birds kept for their eggs and meat

Precise
(pri SYS)
exact

Queasy
(CWEEZY)
feeling of sickness

Rash
careless; rushing; a large number

Ravenous
extremely hungry

Reputation
(rep yuh TAY shun)
how your character is seen by others

"I'm absolutely ravenous. I need some nourishment. I wonder what tasty morsels are in this marquee."

"It´s uncanny! Just the sight of those sundaes makes my mouth full of saliva."

Reside
(ri ZYD)
to live somewhere

Retain
(ri TAYN)
to keep

Revenge
(ri VENJ)
to get your own back for something said or done

Saliva
(suh LY vuh)
spit

Scrumptious
(SCRUM shus)
delicious

Sufficient
(suh FISH unt)
enough for what is needed.

Translate
(trans LAYT)
to change from one language to another

Uncanny
(un CAN i)
mysterious

Utensil
(yoo TEN sil)
a tool used in the kitchen

Vomit
to be sick from the stomach

Crossword

Across:

4. Dark or grim
5. A tube that takes blood from the heart
6. To live somewhere
8. To eat greedily
10. A small piece of food
12. To be sick from the stomach
13. To stop from doing something because you´re not sure

Down:

1. To happen
2. A greedy pig!
3. A crazy person
7. Something you can eat
9. To keep
11. A large number or careless

Word Search

```
A F H J Y U L A V A T O R Y I
S W T C N L B V R A N I L O N
U A H L M U W A C A B O M R G
F Q W R N S Z I N D U L G E R
F A G R I C U L T U R E W P E
I S Q T J I K A Q E T R G U D
C T K F M O D B G T H A T T I
I O I F Q U E L A E G D N A E
E N C L O S E E J T W I M T N
N I A G J K L L P E G C K I T
T S U P R E C I S E H A I O C
H H E Q T R A N S L A T E N A
Y E K A T H E R I N E E Q A B
R D I S A P P R O V E D G T O
A W H N M E G R O T E S Q U E
```

Food

1. Available
2. Agriculture
3. Astonished
4. Disapprove
5. Eradicate
6. Enclose
7. Grotesque
8. Indulge
9. Ingredient
10. Lavatory
11. Luscious
12. Precise
13. Reputation
14. Sufficient
15. Translate

This page is photocopiable for classroom use only.

SECTION 2 - CHECKLIST

1. Artery
- ☐ Understood
- ☐ Used in speech
- ☐ Used in writing

2. Available
- ☐ Understood
- ☐ Used in speech
- ☐ Used in writing

3. Agriculture
- ☐ Understood
- ☐ Used in speech
- ☐ Used in writing

4. Astonished
- ☐ Understood
- ☐ Used in speech
- ☐ Used in writing

5. Bleak
- ☐ Understood
- ☐ Used in speech
- ☐ Used in writing

6. Consumed
- ☐ Understood
- ☐ Used in speech
- ☐ Used in writing

7. Caramel
- ☐ Understood
- ☐ Used in speech
- ☐ Used in writing

8. Dominate
- ☐ Understood
- ☐ Used in speech
- ☐ Used in writing

9. Devour
- ☐ Understood
- ☐ Used in speech
- ☐ Used in writing

10. Dejected
- ☐ Understood
- ☐ Used in speech
- ☐ Used in writing

11. Disapprove
- ☐ Understood
- ☐ Used in speech
- ☐ Used in writing

12. Eradicate
- ☐ Understood
- ☐ Used in speech
- ☐ Used in writing

13. Edible
- ☐ Understood
- ☐ Used in speech
- ☐ Used in writing

14. Exceedingly
- ☐ Understood
- ☐ Used in speech
- ☐ Used in writing

15. Enclose
- ☐ Understood
- ☐ Used in speech
- ☐ Used in writing

16. Falter
- ☐ Understood
- ☐ Used in speech
- ☐ Used in writing

17. Garnished
- ☐ Understood
- ☐ Used in speech
- ☐ Used in writing

18. Glutton
- ☐ Understood
- ☐ Used in speech
- ☐ Used in writing

19. Grotesque
- ☐ Understood
- ☐ Used in speech
- ☐ Used in writing

20. Haul
- ☐ Understood
- ☐ Used in speech
- ☐ Used in writing

21. Heave
- ☐ Understood
- ☐ Used in speech
- ☐ Used in writing

22. Hesitate
- ☐ Understood
- ☐ Used in speech
- ☐ Used in writing

23. Indigestion
- ☐ Understood
- ☐ Used in speech
- ☐ Used in writing

24. Indulge
- ☐ Understood
- ☐ Used in speech
- ☐ Used in writing

25. Ingredient
- ☐ Understood
- ☐ Used in speech
- ☐ Used in writing

26. Intestines
- ☐ Understood
- ☐ Used in speech
- ☐ Used in writing

27. Irresistible
- ☐ Understood
- ☐ Used in speech
- ☐ Used in writing

28. Lavatory
- ☐ Understood
- ☐ Used in speech
- ☐ Used in writing

29. Luscious
- ☐ Understood
- ☐ Used in speech
- ☐ Used in writing

30. Maniac
- ☐ Understood
- ☐ Used in speech
- ☐ Used in writing

31. Marquee
- ☐ Understood
- ☐ Used in speech
- ☐ Used in writing

32. Morsels
- ☐ Understood
- ☐ Used in speech
- ☐ Used in writing

33. Nourishment
- ☐ Understood
- ☐ Used in speech
- ☐ Used in writing

34. Occur
- ☐ Understood
- ☐ Used in speech
- ☐ Used in writing

35. Poultry
- ☐ Understood
- ☐ Used in speech
- ☐ Used in writing

36. Precise
- ☐ Understood
- ☐ Used in speech
- ☐ Used in writing

37. Queasy
- ☐ Understood
- ☐ Used in speech
- ☐ Used in writing

38. Rash
- ☐ Understood
- ☐ Used in speech
- ☐ Used in writing

39. Ravenous
- ☐ Understood
- ☐ Used in speech
- ☐ Used in writing

40. Reputation
- ☐ Understood
- ☐ Used in speech
- ☐ Used in writing

41. Reside
- ☐ Understood
- ☐ Used in speech
- ☐ Used in writing

42. Retain
- ☐ Understood
- ☐ Used in speech
- ☐ Used in writing

43. Revenge
- ☐ Understood
- ☐ Used in speech
- ☐ Used in writing

44. Saliva
- ☐ Understood
- ☐ Used in speech
- ☐ Used in writing

45. Scrumptious
- ☐ Understood
- ☐ Used in speech
- ☐ Used in writing

46. Sufficient
- ☐ Understood
- ☐ Used in speech
- ☐ Used in writing

47. Translate
- ☐ Understood
- ☐ Used in speech
- ☐ Used in writing

48. Uncanny
- ☐ Understood
- ☐ Used in speech
- ☐ Used in writing

49. Utensil
- ☐ Understood
- ☐ Used in speech
- ☐ Used in writing

50. Vomit
- ☐ Understood
- ☐ Used in speech
- ☐ Used in writing

Wondrous Words

Section Three

"These beige corduroys are really durable."

Absolute
(ab suh LOOT)
total

Affluent
wealthy, rich

Approve
(uh PROOV)
to speak of favourably, to agree to

Artificial
(ar ti FISH ul)
not natural, man-made

Beige
(bayzh)
a yellowish-brown colour

Blunder
a serious mistake

Continental
(con tin ENT ul)
European

Corduroy
a cotton material with length ways ribs

Detest
(di TEST)
to hate

Durable
(DIOR ubl)
long lasting

Eccentric
(ec SEN tric)
weird, bizarre, odd

Elegant
(EL i gunt)
excellent manners, style and taste

Embellished
(em BEL isht)
fancied up

Enhanced
(en HANST)
improved

Envious
jealous

Fabricated
made up; made in a factory

Fabulous
incredible; marvellous

Flattery
to over-praise someone in order to achieve something

Galore
(guh LOR)
in a great number

Gape
to stare with your mouth open

"Winnie's already elegant appearance is enhanced and embellished by her beret and fabulous earrings."

"Now that's what I call flattery!"

"Her immaculate look is finished off with an intricately embroidered T shirt, a black skirt and a full navel display."

Hideous
(HID i us)
horrible, frightful, repulsive

Imitate
to copy

Immaculate
(im AC yuh lut)
pure and perfect; spotless; very smart

Intricately
(IN tri cut li)
complicated

Laundry
a place where clothes are washed; pieces of clothing to be washed

Leisure
(LEH zhuh)
free time

Morbid
gloomy; gruesome

Nativity
(nuh TIV iti)
birth, especially the birth of Jesus

Navel
(NAY vul)
your belly button

Obedient
(oh BEE di unt)
you do as you are told

Obscure
(obs KIUR)
unclear; not well-known

Oral
to do with the mouth

Pamper
to treat with extreme care

Parasol
an umbrella for the sun

Pauper
(POR puh)
a very poor person

Persuasion
(per SWAY zhun)
the power to convince someone

Possession
(puh ZESH un)
a thing that you own

Regret
(ri GRET)
to be sorry about something

Resourceful
(ri SORS ful)
skillful in handling situations

Resemble
(ri ZEM bl)
to look like

"In hot weather this parasol is my favourite possession."

"Her stupendous robe comes in a vivid turquoise textile, with a scarlet belt."

Robe
a long flowing dress

Roughage
(RUF ij)
food that is high in fibre

Scarlet
bright red

Scorch
to criticise bitterly; to burn changing the colour;

Stupendous
(stioo PEN dus)
amazing, marvellous

Textile
cloth

Truant
someone absent from school without permission

Turquoise
(TER coiz or TER cwoiz)
a bright greeny-blue colour

Vivid
clear

Umbilical cord
(um bi LY cul)
a tube along which a baby receives nourishment from the mother before birth

Crossword

Across:

1. A very poor person
4. To do with the mouth
7. To treat with extreme care
8. Jealous
9. To hate
11. To stare with the mouth wide open
12. Marvellous
13. Wealthy

Down:

2. To be sorry about something
3. Gloomy; Gruesome
5. Free time
6. To copy
10. In a great number

This page is photocopiable for classroom use only.

Word Search

```
F A P E R Y A R O U G H A G E
A R E S E M B L E A W R T Y B
B R R A W F S A H I D E O U S
R T S B T G O B E D I E N T Q
I B U A W N L R A N I L O N W
C T A Q B U U Q K T T T J A D
A E S C O N T I N E N T A L T
T X I T B A E L I M O Q B T B
E T O B S Q W S C O R C H K A
D I N B C H J K A Q B M R I P
R L R Y U L A U R O H T Q W P
W E E R R E C C E N T R I C R
Q G H R E M O R S E U H W Q O
B K A T H E R I N E A N N E V
A R T I F I C I A L W L Y M E
```

Clothes

1. Absolute
2. Approve
3. Artificial
4. Continental
5. Eccentric
6. Fabricated
7. Hideous
8. Obedient
9. Obscure
10. Persuasion
11. Remorse
12. Resemble
13. Roughage
14. Scorch
15. Textile

35

SECTION 3 - CHECKLIST

1. **Absolute**
   - ☐ Understood
   - ☐ Used in speech
   - ☐ Used in writing

2. **Affluent**
   - ☐ Understood
   - ☐ Used in speech
   - ☐ Used in writing

3. **Approve**
   - ☐ Understood
   - ☐ Used in speech
   - ☐ Used in writing

4. **Artificial**
   - ☐ Understood
   - ☐ Used in speech
   - ☐ Used in writing

5. **Beige**
   - ☐ Understood
   - ☐ Used in speech
   - ☐ Used in writing

6. **Blunder**
   - ☐ Understood
   - ☐ Used in speech
   - ☐ Used in writing

7. **Continental**
   - ☐ Understood
   - ☐ Used in speech
   - ☐ Used in writing

8. **Corduroy**
   - ☐ Understood
   - ☐ Used in speech
   - ☐ Used in writing

9. **Detest**
   - ☐ Understood
   - ☐ Used in speech
   - ☐ Used in writing

10. **Durable**
    - ☐ Understood
    - ☐ Used in speech
    - ☐ Used in writing

11. **Eccentric**
    - ☐ Understood
    - ☐ Used in speech
    - ☐ Used in writing

12. **Elegant**
    - ☐ Understood
    - ☐ Used in speech
    - ☐ Used in writing

13. **Embellished**
    - ☐ Understood
    - ☐ Used in speech
    - ☐ Used in writing

14. **Enhanced**
    - ☐ Understood
    - ☐ Used in speech
    - ☐ Used in writing

15. **Envious**
    - ☐ Understood
    - ☐ Used in speech
    - ☐ Used in writing

16. **Fabricated**
    - ☐ Understood
    - ☐ Used in speech
    - ☐ Used in writing

17. **Fabulous**
    - ☐ Understood
    - ☐ Used in speech
    - ☐ Used in writing

18. **Flattery**
    - ☐ Understood
    - ☐ Used in speech
    - ☐ Used in writing

19. **Galore**
    - ☐ Understood
    - ☐ Used in speech
    - ☐ Used in writing

20. **Gape**
    - ☐ Understood
    - ☐ Used in speech
    - ☐ Used in writing

21. **Hideous**
    - ☐ Understood
    - ☐ Used in speech
    - ☐ Used in writing

22. **Imitate**
    - ☐ Understood
    - ☐ Used in speech
    - ☐ Used in writing

23. **Immaculate**
    - ☐ Understood
    - ☐ Used in speech
    - ☐ Used in writing

24. **Intricately**
    - ☐ Understood
    - ☐ Used in speech
    - ☐ Used in writing

25. **Laundry**
    - ☐ Understood
    - ☐ Used in speech
    - ☐ Used in writing

26. **Leisure**
    - ☐ Understood
    - ☐ Used in speech
    - ☐ Used in writing

27. **Morbid**
    - ☐ Understood
    - ☐ Used in speech
    - ☐ Used in writing

28. **Nativity**
    - ☐ Understood
    - ☐ Used in speech
    - ☐ Used in writing

29. **Navel**
    - ☐ Understood
    - ☐ Used in speech
    - ☐ Used in writing

30. **Obedient**
    - ☐ Understood
    - ☐ Used in speech
    - ☐ Used in writing

31. **Obscure**
    - ☐ Understood
    - ☐ Used in speech
    - ☐ Used in writing

32. **Oral**
    - ☐ Understood
    - ☐ Used in speech
    - ☐ Used in writing

33. **Pamper**
    - ☐ Understood
    - ☐ Used in speech
    - ☐ Used in writing

34. **Parasol**
    - ☐ Understood
    - ☐ Used in speech
    - ☐ Used in writing

35. **Pauper**
    - ☐ Understood
    - ☐ Used in speech
    - ☐ Used in writing

36. **Persuasion**
    - ☐ Understood
    - ☐ Used in speech
    - ☐ Used in writing

37. **Possession**
    - ☐ Understood
    - ☐ Used in speech
    - ☐ Used in writing

38. **Regret**
    - ☐ Understood
    - ☐ Used in speech
    - ☐ Used in writing

39. **Resourceful**
    - ☐ Understood
    - ☐ Used in speech
    - ☐ Used in writing

40. **Roughage**
    - ☐ Understood
    - ☐ Used in speech
    - ☐ Used in writing

41. **Robe**
    - ☐ Understood
    - ☐ Used in speech
    - ☐ Used in writing

42. **Resemble**
    - ☐ Understood
    - ☐ Used in speech
    - ☐ Used in writing

43. **Scarlet**
    - ☐ Understood
    - ☐ Used in speech
    - ☐ Used in writing

44. **Scorch**
    - ☐ Understood
    - ☐ Used in speech
    - ☐ Used in writing

45. **Stupendous**
    - ☐ Understood
    - ☐ Used in speech
    - ☐ Used in writing

46. **Textile**
    - ☐ Understood
    - ☐ Used in speech
    - ☐ Used in writing

47. **Truant**
    - ☐ Understood
    - ☐ Used in speech
    - ☐ Used in writing

48. **Turquoise**
    - ☐ Understood
    - ☐ Used in speech
    - ☐ Used in writing

49. **Vivid**
    - ☐ Understood
    - ☐ Used in speech
    - ☐ Used in writing

50. **Umbilical cord**
    - ☐ Understood
    - ☐ Used in speech
    - ☐ Used in writing

Wondrous Words

Section Four

"In the aquarium some fish ascend while others descend."

Agile
(AJ eil)
able to move quickly and easily

Aquarium
(uh CWAIR ri um)
a tank for keeping fish and plants

Appalling
(uh POR ling)
causing horror, frightening

Approximate
(uh PROX im ut)
nearly correct, close to

Ascend
(uh SEND)
to go up

Camouflage
(KAM uh flarzh)
hidden through disguise

Combat
a fight; to fight

Curiosity
(ci or i OS iti)
a wanting to learn or know

Delete
(di LEET)
to erase, rub out

Descend
(di SEND)
to go down

Dialogue
(DY uh log)
a conversation

Dispute
(DISP yoot or
disp YOOT)
an angry argument; to argue angrily

Dwell
to live in a place

Equipped
(i CWIPT)
supplied with all the needed things

Exceptionally
(ex SEP shun uli)
extremely

Ferocious
(fuh ROH shus)
extremely fierce and violent

Financial
(fy NAN shul)
dealing with money

Fret
to worry

Generation
(jen uh RAY shun)
a group of people born about the same time

Gesture
(JEST yuh)
an expression, a signal or to signal

"Some creatures are exceptionally ferocious!"

"Some animals just eat plants. They are called herbivores."

Harshly
roughly; unpleasantly

Herbivores
plant-eating animals

Hypnotise
(HIP nuh teiz)
to bring someone under your spell

Ignite
(ig NYT)
to catch fire

Illuminate
(i LOO min ayt)
to light up

Immature
(im ut YOR)
lacking mental and physical growth

Instalment
(in STORL munt)
a stage of payment of a debt; a part of a story

Intend
(in TEND)
to mean to

Mongrel
(MUNG rul)
a dog of mixed breeds

Mystify
(MIS ti fy)
to confuse or perplex

Numerous
(NIOO muh rus)
many

Quadruple
(cwod ROO pl)
to make four times bigger

Pasture
(PAST yuh)
a field for animals to graze

Pedigree
an animal of pure breed

Plumage
(PLOOM ij)
feathers

Predators
(PRED uh tuz)
creatures of prey; those that live by exploiting and robbing others

Prey
(PRAY)
an animal that is hunted; to make raids on; to have a distressing effect

Pursue
(puh SIOO)
to follow

Reek
a stink; to stink

Reproduce
(ree prud YOOS)
to make babies

"Whether it´s predators or prey, they all reproduce!"

"A tarantula is not a vertebrate but a stallion is."

Scarce
(scairs)
in short supply; few in number

Seething
to be really angry

Stallion
a male adult horse

Talisman
a lucky charm

Tarantula
(tuh RANT yul uh)
a huge hairy spider

Twilight
(TWY lyt)
the time of day when it is neither light or dark

Unicorn
(YOO ni corn)
a mythical creature which is a horse with a horn growing from its forehead

Venom
poison

Vermin
lice, rats or any other harmful creatures; an offensive person

Vertebrate
(VER tuh brut)
a backbone; the large group of animals with a backbone

Crossword

Across:

5	In short supply
6	Dusk
8	To worry
9	To mean to
11	Poison
12	To live
13	An animal of pure breed

Down:

1	To confuse
2	A field of grass to be eaten
3	A dreadful smell!
4	Quick moving
7	Roughly, unpleasantly
9	To catch fire
10	To erase

Word Search

```
H Y G E N E R A T I O N A R Q
I P J K U Q N P L U M A G E U
H U K A M V O P D E N S I N A
I R Q E E T U A G A I M E E D
L S Y A R B N L A N G E L L R
L U N B O N Q L E E H U K L U
U E T U U E D I A L O G U E P
M M O P S B M N A Q N T Y M L
I L C A B O P G E S T U R E E
N A V A N S E E T H I N G A A
A N E S R A N I L O C A B O M
T Q R C R T U I M M A T U R E
E B M E K A T H E R I N E A N
N K I N Q U N I C O R N A B M
A Z N D E S C E N D U I O P M
```

Animals
1. Appalling
2. Ascend
3. Descend
4. Dialogue
5. Generation
6. Gesture
7. Illuminate
8. Immature
9. Numerous
10. Quadruple
11. Plumage
12. Pursue
13. Seething
14. Unicorn
15. Vermin

This page is photocopiable for classroom use only.

SECTION 4 - CHECKLIST

1. Agile
- ☐ Understood
- ☐ Used in speech
- ☐ Used in writing

2. Aquarium
- ☐ Understood
- ☐ Used in speech
- ☐ Used in writing

3. Appalling
- ☐ Understood
- ☐ Used in speech
- ☐ Used in writing

4. Approximate
- ☐ Understood
- ☐ Used in speech
- ☐ Used in writing

5. Ascend
- ☐ Understood
- ☐ Used in speech
- ☐ Used in writing

6. Camouflage
- ☐ Understood
- ☐ Used in speech
- ☐ Used in writing

7. Combat
- ☐ Understood
- ☐ Used in speech
- ☐ Used in writing

8. Curiosity
- ☐ Understood
- ☐ Used in speech
- ☐ Used in writing

9. Delete
- ☐ Understood
- ☐ Used in speech
- ☐ Used in writing

10. Descend
- ☐ Understood
- ☐ Used in speech
- ☐ Used in writing

11. Dialogue
- ☐ Understood
- ☐ Used in speech
- ☐ Used in writing

12. Dispute
- ☐ Understood
- ☐ Used in speech
- ☐ Used in writing

13. Dwell
- ☐ Understood
- ☐ Used in speech
- ☐ Used in writing

14. Equipped
- ☐ Understood
- ☐ Used in speech
- ☐ Used in writing

15. Exceptionally
- ☐ Understood
- ☐ Used in speech
- ☐ Used in writing

16. Ferocious
- ☐ Understood
- ☐ Used in speech
- ☐ Used in writing

17. Financial
- ☐ Understood
- ☐ Used in speech
- ☐ Used in writing

18. Fret
- ☐ Understood
- ☐ Used in speech
- ☐ Used in writing

19. Generation
- ☐ Understood
- ☐ Used in speech
- ☐ Used in writing

20. Gesture
- ☐ Understood
- ☐ Used in speech
- ☐ Used in writing

21. Harshly
- ☐ Understood
- ☐ Used in speech
- ☐ Used in writing

22. Herbivores
- ☐ Understood
- ☐ Used in speech
- ☐ Used in writing

23. Hypnotise
- ☐ Understood
- ☐ Used in speech
- ☐ Used in writing

24. Ignite
- ☐ Understood
- ☐ Used in speech
- ☐ Used in writing

25. Illuminate
- ☐ Understood
- ☐ Used in speech
- ☐ Used in writing

26. Immature
- ☐ Understood
- ☐ Used in speech
- ☐ Used in writing

27. Installment
- ☐ Understood
- ☐ Used in speech
- ☐ Used in writing

28. Intend
- ☐ Understood
- ☐ Used in speech
- ☐ Used in writing

29. Mongrel
- ☐ Understood
- ☐ Used in speech
- ☐ Used in writing

30. Mystify
- ☐ Understood
- ☐ Used in speech
- ☐ Used in writing

31. Numerous
- ☐ Understood
- ☐ Used in speech
- ☐ Used in writing

32. Quadruple
- ☐ Understood
- ☐ Used in speech
- ☐ Used in writing

33. Pasture
- ☐ Understood
- ☐ Used in speech
- ☐ Used in writing

34. Pedigree
- ☐ Understood
- ☐ Used in speech
- ☐ Used in writing

35. Plumage
- ☐ Understood
- ☐ Used in speech
- ☐ Used in writing

36. Predators
- ☐ Understood
- ☐ Used in speech
- ☐ Used in writing

37. Prey
- ☐ Understood
- ☐ Used in speech
- ☐ Used in writing

38. Persue
- ☐ Understood
- ☐ Used in speech
- ☐ Used in writing

39. Reek
- ☐ Understood
- ☐ Used in speech
- ☐ Used in writing

40. Reproduce
- ☐ Understood
- ☐ Used in speech
- ☐ Used in writing

41. Scarce
- ☐ Understood
- ☐ Used in speech
- ☐ Used in writing

42. Seething
- ☐ Understood
- ☐ Used in speech
- ☐ Used in writing

43. Stallion
- ☐ Understood
- ☐ Used in speech
- ☐ Used in writing

44. Talisman
- ☐ Understood
- ☐ Used in speech
- ☐ Used in writing

45. Tarantula
- ☐ Understood
- ☐ Used in speech
- ☐ Used in writing

46. Twilight
- ☐ Understood
- ☐ Used in speech
- ☐ Used in writing

47. Unicorn
- ☐ Understood
- ☐ Used in speech
- ☐ Used in writing

48. Venom
- ☐ Understood
- ☐ Used in speech
- ☐ Used in writing

49. Vermin
- ☐ Understood
- ☐ Used in speech
- ☐ Used in writing

50. Vertebrate
- ☐ Understood
- ☐ Used in speech
- ☐ Used in writing

Wondrous Words

Section Five

Biography - a book of a person´s life
Autobiography - a person´s life story written by him or her.

Abandoned
(uh BAN dund)
something given up; left

Abbreviated
(uh BREE vi ayt ud)
shortened

Amateur
(AM uh tuh)
a person who does any activity for pleasure, rather than being paid

Atrocious
(uh TROH shus)
extremely wicked; shockingly bad

Autobiography
(ort oh by OG ru fi)
a person´s life story written by him or her

Biography
(by OG ru fi)
a book of a person´s life

Circumstance
situations

Content
(con TENT)
happy; satisfied

Devastate
to ruin; to destroy

Eager
(EE guh)
enthusiastic

Eliminate
(ee LIM in ayt)
to get rid of

Epidemic
(epi DEM ic)
a disease which spreads and affects many people

Exhale
(ex HAYL)
to breathe out

Exhaustion
(eg ZORST yun)
completely tired out

Fatigue
(fuh TEEG)
tiredness

Feeble
weak

Gash
a deep, long cut in the flesh

Gravely
(GRAY vli)
seriously

Hooligan
a rough and violent person

Horrendous
(huh REND us)
dreadful, horrible

"The feeble boxer was suffering from exhaustion and fatigue. He had been gravely injured in round 3, suffering a horrendous gash under his right eye."

"The more melanin you have, the darker your skin."

Illegal
(il EE gul)
against the law

Inconvenient
(in con VEE ni unt)
causing difficulty, not suitable

Inhale
(in HAYL)
to breathe in

Lethal
(LEE thul)
deadly

Logo
(LOH go)
a distinctive company symbol

Melanin
a pigment that makes you brown skinned

Motivation
(moh ti VAY shun)
the cause that makes someone do something

Motto
a short phrase that sums up the meaning or intension of a group or institution

Negotiate
(ni GO shi ayt)
to make a deal

Opponent
(uh POH nunt)
the opposition in a fight or game

Permanent
lasting a very long time

Perspire
(pers PYR)
to sweat

Prevent
(pri VENT)
to stop

Previous
(PREE vi us)
at an earlier time; the one before

Request
(ri CWEST)
to ask for something; something asked for

Respiration
(res pi RAY shun)
the act of breathing

Rigorous
thorough, very strict

Rile
to make angry

Salary
a fixed payment for work done

Sensational
(sen SAY shun ul)
exceptionally impressive

"Young ladies don´t sweat, they perspire!"

At the Nou Camp **venue**, in the Barcelona **versus** Real Madrid game, the last **substitute** scored the winning goal. Barcelona **triumph** again!

Severe
(siv EER)
serious; harsh in punishment

Substitute
to change one thing for another; a person or thing used in place of another

Tantrum
a fit of childish bad temper

Temporary
(TEM puh ruh ri)
just for a short while

Triumph
(TRY umf)
the celebration of victory

Ultimate
(UL tim ut)
last; the highest point

Umpire
a referee in some sports

Venue
(VEN yoo)
the site where something takes place

Versus
against

Wretched
(RECH id)
miserable, pitiful

50

Crossword

Across:

1. What you are paid regularly
2. To make angry
4. Miserable, pitiful
5. To breathe in
8. A symbol
9. To breathe out
10. A short phrase expressing the purpose of a person, city or company
11. Against the law
12. To ask for

Down:

1. Strict, harsh
3. A referee in some sports
6. The opposite to a professional
7. Happy and satisfied

Word Search

R A B T M O T I V A T I O N D
K U A K A T H E R I N E N H E
P R E B N P R E V I O U S O V
R A F H A E A G Y T U B I O A
E L I M I N A T E R T T K L S
V X V B T J D A K T S A A I T
E T J K L S T O E I O H G G A
N B O P P O N E N T T D T A T
T T E G H J K C E E T H U N E
W Q A Q E R H J L N D A W R B
A W G S E N S A T I O N A L T
G T E E F N E G O T I A T E Y
C I R C U M S T A N C E S L J
T Y I G H A T E M P O R A R Y
T P E R M A N E N T A Y E H T

Sports
1. Abandoned
2. Circumstances
3. Devastate
4. Eager
5. Eliminate
6. Hooligan
7. Lethal
8. Motivation
9. Negotiate
10. Opponent
11. Permanent
12. Prevent
13. Previous
14. Sensational
15. Temporary

This page is photocopiable for classroom use only.

SECTION 5 - CHECKLIST

1. Abandoned
   - ☐ Understood
   - ☐ Used in speech
   - ☐ Used in writing

2. Abbreviated
   - ☐ Understood
   - ☐ Used in speech
   - ☐ Used in writing

3. Amateur
   - ☐ Understood
   - ☐ Used in speech
   - ☐ Used in writing

4. Atrocious
   - ☐ Understood
   - ☐ Used in speech
   - ☐ Used in writing

5. Autobiography
   - ☐ Understood
   - ☐ Used in speech
   - ☐ Used in writing

6. Biography
   - ☐ Understood
   - ☐ Used in speech
   - ☐ Used in writing

7. Circumstances
   - ☐ Understood
   - ☐ Used in speech
   - ☐ Used in writing

8. Content
   - ☐ Understood
   - ☐ Used in speech
   - ☐ Used in writing

9. Devestate
   - ☐ Understood
   - ☐ Used in speech
   - ☐ Used in writing

10. Eager
    - ☐ Understood
    - ☐ Used in speech
    - ☐ Used in writing

11. Eliminate
    - ☐ Understood
    - ☐ Used in speech
    - ☐ Used in writing

12. Epidemic
    - ☐ Understood
    - ☐ Used in speech
    - ☐ Used in writing

13. Exhale
    - ☐ Understood
    - ☐ Used in speech
    - ☐ Used in writing

14. Exhaustion
    - ☐ Understood
    - ☐ Used in speech
    - ☐ Used in writing

15. Fatigue
    - ☐ Understood
    - ☐ Used in speech
    - ☐ Used in writing

16. Feeble
    - ☐ Understood
    - ☐ Used in speech
    - ☐ Used in writing

17. Gash
    - ☐ Understood
    - ☐ Used in speech
    - ☐ Used in writing

18. Gravely
    - ☐ Understood
    - ☐ Used in speech
    - ☐ Used in writing

19. Hooligan
    - ☐ Understood
    - ☐ Used in speech
    - ☐ Used in writing

20. Horrendous
    - ☐ Understood
    - ☐ Used in speech
    - ☐ Used in writing

21. Illegal
    - ☐ Understood
    - ☐ Used in speech
    - ☐ Used in writing

22. Inconvenient
    - ☐ Understood
    - ☐ Used in speech
    - ☐ Used in writing

23. Inhale
    - ☐ Understood
    - ☐ Used in speech
    - ☐ Used in writing

24. Lethal
    - ☐ Understood
    - ☐ Used in speech
    - ☐ Used in writing

25. Logo
    - ☐ Understood
    - ☐ Used in speech
    - ☐ Used in writing

26. Melanin
    - ☐ Understood
    - ☐ Used in speech
    - ☐ Used in writing

27. Motivation
    - ☐ Understood
    - ☐ Used in speech
    - ☐ Used in writing

28. Motto
    - ☐ Understood
    - ☐ Used in speech
    - ☐ Used in writing

29. Negotiate
    - ☐ Understood
    - ☐ Used in speech
    - ☐ Used in writing

30. Opponent
    - ☐ Understood
    - ☐ Used in speech
    - ☐ Used in writing

31. Permanent
    - ☐ Understood
    - ☐ Used in speech
    - ☐ Used in writing

32. Perspire
    - ☐ Understood
    - ☐ Used in speech
    - ☐ Used in writing

33. Prevent
    - ☐ Understood
    - ☐ Used in speech
    - ☐ Used in writing

34. Previous
    - ☐ Understood
    - ☐ Used in speech
    - ☐ Used in writing

35. Request
    - ☐ Understood
    - ☐ Used in speech
    - ☐ Used in writing

36. Respiration
    - ☐ Understood
    - ☐ Used in speech
    - ☐ Used in writing

37. Rigorous
    - ☐ Understood
    - ☐ Used in speech
    - ☐ Used in writing

38. Rile
    - ☐ Understood
    - ☐ Used in speech
    - ☐ Used in writing

39. Salary
    - ☐ Understood
    - ☐ Used in speech
    - ☐ Used in writing

40. Sensational
    - ☐ Understood
    - ☐ Used in speech
    - ☐ Used in writing

41. Severe
    - ☐ Understood
    - ☐ Used in speech
    - ☐ Used in writing

42. Substitute
    - ☐ Understood
    - ☐ Used in speech
    - ☐ Used in writing

43. Tantrum
    - ☐ Understood
    - ☐ Used in speech
    - ☐ Used in writing

44. Temporary
    - ☐ Understood
    - ☐ Used in speech
    - ☐ Used in writing

45. Triumph
    - ☐ Understood
    - ☐ Used in speech
    - ☐ Used in writing

46. Ultimate
    - ☐ Understood
    - ☐ Used in speech
    - ☐ Used in writing

47. Umpire
    - ☐ Understood
    - ☐ Used in speech
    - ☐ Used in writing

48. Venue
    - ☐ Understood
    - ☐ Used in speech
    - ☐ Used in writing

49. Versus
    - ☐ Understood
    - ☐ Used in speech
    - ☐ Used in writing

50. Wretched
    - ☐ Understood
    - ☐ Used in speech
    - ☐ Used in writing

Wondrous Words

Section Six

The chauffeur was accustomed to accelerating abruptly to avoid any collision.

Abruptly
(uh BRUPT li)
suddenly

Accelerate
(ac SEL uh rayt)
to increase speed

Accustomed
(uh CUS tumd)
to be used to something

Acquire
(uh CWY er)
to get

Brittle
easily broken or cracked

Chauffeur
(SHOH fer or show FER)
a person employed as a driver

Collision
(cuh LIZH un)
a crash

Conceal
(con SEEL)
to hide

Construct
(con STRUCT)
to build

Contestant
(con TEST unt)
someone taking part in a competition

Defect
(DEE fect)
a fault

Detect
(di TECT)
to discover, to uncover, to find

Efficient
(i FISH unt)
working very well but without much or any waste or cost

Enchanting
(en CHAN ting)
being brought under a spell; delightful

Excursion
(ex CER shun)
a short trip

Fragment
a small piece broken off

Glimpse
a quick look

Gravity
seriousness; the force that brings things down in the Earth´s atmosphere

Hospitable
(hos PIT ubl)
offering a generous and friendly welcome

Host/Hostess
a man or woman who receives guests and entertains them

On our long flight with this airline the hostesses were extremely hospitable and really efficient.

55

"A **momentous** development was the **manufacture** of trains and ships on a large scale."

Inconsistent
(in cun SIS tunt)
changeable

Inefficient
(in i FISH unt)
does not work very well

Inevitable
(in EV it ubl)
cannot be avoided

Inhospitable
(in hos PIT ubl)
not friendly and welcoming

Interior
(in TEER i uh)
the inside

Lithe
(lyth)
bendy

Manufacture
(man yoo FACT yuh)
making things on a large scale in factories

Momentous
(moh MEN tus)
very important

Muffle
to deaden a sound

Nimble
quick, light and easy in movement and thought

Obtained
(ob TAYND)
got

Perimeter
(puh RIM it uh)
the length of the boundary outside something.

Periscope
an instrument for viewing around objects with mirrors

Perplex
(per PLECS)
to puzzle

Posterior
(pos TEER i uh)
the human bottom

Predict
(pri DICT)
to foretell

Rapidly
quickly

Require
to need

Retail
(REE tayl)
to sell

Rotating
turning around, spinning

"I am perplexed where you obtained that rapidly rotating periscope!"

57

"The rickety old bike barely reached the summit, but then would surge down the mountain at a terrific speed."

Rickety
shaky

Stethoscope
an instrument to find the sounds in the body

Summit
the highest point, the peak

Superior
(soo PEER ri uh)
someone of higher rank; greater in quality

Surge
a strong movement forwards

Titter
to giggle quietly

Tranquil
(TRAN cwil)
peaceful

Translucent
(trans LOO sunt)
lets light through but not see-through

Unconscious
(un CON shus)
not being aware; being knocked out

Zeppelin
a cigar-shaped German airship from the 1920s and 30s

Crossword

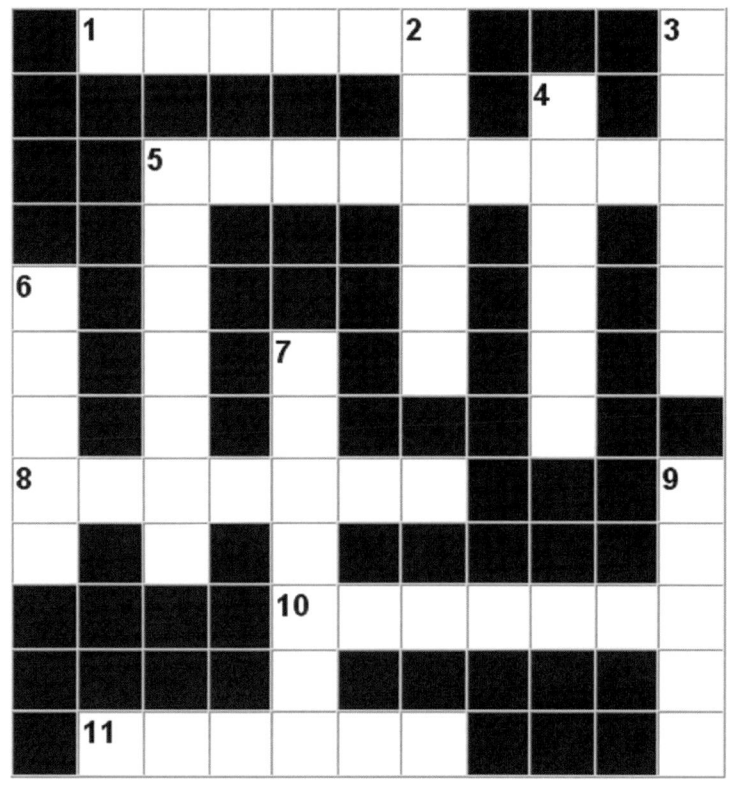

Across:
1. A fault
5. To build
8. It keeps everything on Earth
10. To say what's going to happen
11. To discover

Down:
2. To laugh quietly
3. To sell
4. To deaden a sound
5. To hide
6. A strong movement forwards
7. A quick look
9. Bendy

Word Search

```
F E X C U R S I O N A E H P A
R G H B R I T T L E E H Y E N
N I M B L E E T U N R R T R N
T T A W U T T T Y C V U I S E
I R R T N U H G G H N Y N O D
N A T J C B O F R A G M E N T
E N F R O I S E R N E R F N R
V S J F N N C Y K T A R F E A
I L L S S T O Y K I W Y I L N
T U O A C E P U J N J E C C Q
A C Q U I R E B H G T A I A U
B E O U O I A W T N M T E B I
L N F T U O T U N T Y F N O L
E T S G S R A N I L O T T G M
F T D B A P E D E S T R I A N
```

Transport
1. Acquire
2. Brittle
3. Enchanting
4. Excursion
5. Fragment
6. Inefficient
7. Inevitable
8. Interior
9. Nimble
10. Pedestrian
11. Personnel
12. Stethoscope
13. Tranquil
14. Translucent
15. Unconscious

This page is photocopiable for classroom use only.

SECTION 6 - CHECKLIST

1. Abruptly
   - ☐ Understood
   - ☐ Used in speech
   - ☐ Used in writing

2. Accelerate
   - ☐ Understood
   - ☐ Used in speech
   - ☐ Used in writing

3. Accustomed
   - ☐ Understood
   - ☐ Used in speech
   - ☐ Used in writing

4. Acquire
   - ☐ Understood
   - ☐ Used in speech
   - ☐ Used in writing

5. Brittle
   - ☐ Understood
   - ☐ Used in speech
   - ☐ Used in writing

6. Chauffeur
   - ☐ Understood
   - ☐ Used in speech
   - ☐ Used in writing

7. Collision
   - ☐ Understood
   - ☐ Used in speech
   - ☐ Used in writing

8. Conceal
   - ☐ Understood
   - ☐ Used in speech
   - ☐ Used in writing

9. Construct
   - ☐ Understood
   - ☐ Used in speech
   - ☐ Used in writing

10. Contestant
    - ☐ Understood
    - ☐ Used in speech
    - ☐ Used in writing

11. Defect
    - ☐ Understood
    - ☐ Used in speech
    - ☐ Used in writing

12. Detect
    - ☐ Understood
    - ☐ Used in speech
    - ☐ Used in writing

13. Efficient
    - ☐ Understood
    - ☐ Used in speech
    - ☐ Used in writing

14. Enchanting
    - ☐ Understood
    - ☐ Used in speech
    - ☐ Used in writing

15. Excursion
    - ☐ Understood
    - ☐ Used in speech
    - ☐ Used in writing

16. Fragment
    - ☐ Understood
    - ☐ Used in speech
    - ☐ Used in writing

17. Glimpse
    - ☐ Understood
    - ☐ Used in speech
    - ☐ Used in writing

18. Gravity
    - ☐ Understood
    - ☐ Used in speech
    - ☐ Used in writing

19. Hospitable
    - ☐ Understood
    - ☐ Used in speech
    - ☐ Used in writing

20. Host/Hostess
    - ☐ Understood
    - ☐ Used in speech
    - ☐ Used in writing

21. Inconsistent
    - ☐ Understood
    - ☐ Used in speech
    - ☐ Used in writing

22. Inefficient
    - ☐ Understood
    - ☐ Used in speech
    - ☐ Used in writing

23. Inevitable
    - ☐ Understood
    - ☐ Used in speech
    - ☐ Used in writing

24. Inhospitable
    - ☐ Understood
    - ☐ Used in speech
    - ☐ Used in writing

25. Interior
    - ☐ Understood
    - ☐ Used in speech
    - ☐ Used in writing

26. Lithe
    - ☐ Understood
    - ☐ Used in speech
    - ☐ Used in writing

27. Manufacture
    - ☐ Understood
    - ☐ Used in speech
    - ☐ Used in writing

28. Momentous
    - ☐ Understood
    - ☐ Used in speech
    - ☐ Used in writing

29. Muffle
    - ☐ Understood
    - ☐ Used in speech
    - ☐ Used in writing

30. Nimble
    - ☐ Understood
    - ☐ Used in speech
    - ☐ Used in writing

31. Obtained
    - ☐ Understood
    - ☐ Used in speech
    - ☐ Used in writing

32. Perimeter
    - ☐ Understood
    - ☐ Used in speech
    - ☐ Used in writing

33. Periscope
    - ☐ Understood
    - ☐ Used in speech
    - ☐ Used in writing

34. Perplex
    - ☐ Understood
    - ☐ Used in speech
    - ☐ Used in writing

35. Posterior
    - ☐ Understood
    - ☐ Used in speech
    - ☐ Used in writing

36. Predict
    - ☐ Understood
    - ☐ Used in speech
    - ☐ Used in writing

37. Rapidly
    - ☐ Understood
    - ☐ Used in speech
    - ☐ Used in writing

38. Require
    - ☐ Understood
    - ☐ Used in speech
    - ☐ Used in writing

39. Retail
    - ☐ Understood
    - ☐ Used in speech
    - ☐ Used in writing

40. Rotating
    - ☐ Understood
    - ☐ Used in speech
    - ☐ Used in writing

41. Rickety
    - ☐ Understood
    - ☐ Used in speech
    - ☐ Used in writing

42. Stethoscope
    - ☐ Understood
    - ☐ Used in speech
    - ☐ Used in writing

43. Summit
    - ☐ Understood
    - ☐ Used in speech
    - ☐ Used in writing

44. Superior
    - ☐ Understood
    - ☐ Used in speech
    - ☐ Used in writing

45. Surge
    - ☐ Understood
    - ☐ Used in speech
    - ☐ Used in writing

46. Titter
    - ☐ Understood
    - ☐ Used in speech
    - ☐ Used in writing

47. Tranquil
    - ☐ Understood
    - ☐ Used in speech
    - ☐ Used in writing

48. Translucent
    - ☐ Understood
    - ☐ Used in speech
    - ☐ Used in writing

49. Unconscious
    - ☐ Understood
    - ☐ Used in speech
    - ☐ Used in writing

50. Zeppelin
    - ☐ Understood
    - ☐ Used in speech
    - ☐ Used in writing

Wondrous Words

Section Seven

"The Western Desert is baking hot and extremely arid."

Abolish
(uh BOL ish)
to do away with a law or custom

Adhesive
(ad EE ziv)
glue

Arid
extremely dry with little vegetation

Cease
(sees)
to end

Dastardly
(DAS tud li)
cowardly, mean or sneaky

Diligent
careful; hard-working

Dilute
(dy LOOT)
to add water to a drink to make it less strong

Disintegrate
(dis IN tig rayt)
to break up into tiny pieces

Emigrate
to leave a country to settle in another

Evacuate
(i VAC yoo ayt)
to empty, abandon

62

Eventually
(i VEN tiuh li)
finally

Ghastly
terrifying; extremely unpleasant

Grasp
to hold tightly; to understand

Hemisphere
half of the Earth – top or bottom

Hobbled
walked with difficulty because of an injury

Incidentally
(in sid ENT li)
by the way

Impudent
(IMP yuh dunt)
cheeky

Inhabitant
(in HAB it unt)
someone who lives in a certain place

Insist
(in SIST)
to say or do again and again

Intrepid
(in TREP id)
fearless, adventurous, brave

"Eventually the intrepid explorers hobbled back to base-camp."

63

"Spring comes late this far north. The frozen, pallid sky persists until May."

Liberate
to set free

Lope
to walk with long strides

Manicure
treatment of the hands and fingernails

Merely
(MEER li)
only

Oasis
(oh AY sis)
a fertile, green area in the desert

Opportunity
(op ut YOO ni ti)
an occasion, a chance

Pallid
(PAL id)
pale

Perilous
dangerous

Perpetual
(puh PET yoo ul)
never-ending

Persist
(puh SIST)
to last; to keep on saying or doing something

Pharmacy
(FAR muh si)
a chemist´s

Plead
to beg

Pledge
a promise; to promise

Procession
(pruh SESH un)
an organised parade in the streets

Ramble
to wander aimlessly; to talk or write in a disconnected way

Precipitation
(pri sip ee TAY shun)
rainfall, sleet or snow

Referendum
(ref uh REN dum)
a public vote

Reservoir
(REZ uv war)
a man-made lake of water

Sapphire
(SA fyr)
a blue gem

Scald
(scold)
to get burned by boiling water

"In the autumn the intense precipitation soon fills up the reservoirs."

"The Earth's tilt brings the seasons but does not affect the tropics much. They're always hot!"

Scapegoat
person blamed for the fault of others

Sheer
complete; going down very steeply

Structure
(STRUCT yuh)
a building or a tower

Tragedy
(TRAJ uh di)
a disastrous event

Tropics
regions north and south of the equator

Trinket
something of little value; a cheap decoration

Trespass
to unlawfully enter someone's land

Vertigo
dizziness

Tilt
to lean to one side

Wreath
(reeth)
a circular decoration of vegetation and flowers for Christmas and funerals

Crossword

Across:
- 2 Dangerous
- 5 Going straight down
- 7 To beg
- 8 To understand; to hold tightly
- 9 A green area in the desert
- 12 To walk or talk on and on
- 13 To water down a drink

Down:
- 1 Only
- 2 To promise or a promise
- 3 To say again and again
- 4 To stride out
- 6 Finally
- 10 To get burned by boiling water
- 11 To stop

Word Search

```
R E E V A C U A T E A S T L Y
S A P P H I R E J P I Y L I B
A V S Q T M R I G H A S T L Y
H E M I S P H E R E F I L P P
U R T T W U D A V I D D I H E
R T I D A D S R T Y I A N A R
E I T E M E A B O L I S H R P
V G T L Y N A K O M I T A M E
R O T I I T Y T I Y U A B A T
R I D G J O C E L Y N R I C U
A D H E S I V E E R A D T Y A
I B A N T Y Y U U M T L A U L
B L L T R Q R T K L L Y N P Y
O P P O R T U N I T Y K T U P
N U T U E M I G R A T E T I O
```

The Earth
1. Abolish
2. Adhesive
3. Dastardly
4. Diligent
5. Emigrate
6. Evacuate
7. Ghastly
8. Hemisphere
9. Impudent
10. Inhabitant
11. Opportunity
12. Perpetual
13. Pharmacy
14. Sapphire
15. Vertigo

This page is photocopiable for classroom use only.

SECTION 7 - CHECKLIST

1. Abolish
- ☐ Understood
- ☐ Used in speech
- ☐ Used in writing

2. Adhesive
- ☐ Understood
- ☐ Used in speech
- ☐ Used in writing

3. Arid
- ☐ Understood
- ☐ Used in speech
- ☐ Used in writing

4. Cease
- ☐ Understood
- ☐ Used in speech
- ☐ Used in writing

5. Dastardly
- ☐ Understood
- ☐ Used in speech
- ☐ Used in writing

6. Diligent
- ☐ Understood
- ☐ Used in speech
- ☐ Used in writing

7. Dilute
- ☐ Understood
- ☐ Used in speech
- ☐ Used in writing

8. Disintegrate
- ☐ Understood
- ☐ Used in speech
- ☐ Used in writing

9. Emigrate
- ☐ Understood
- ☐ Used in speech
- ☐ Used in writing

10. Evacuate
- ☐ Understood
- ☐ Used in speech
- ☐ Used in writing

11. Eventually
- ☐ Understood
- ☐ Used in speech
- ☐ Used in writing

12. Ghastly
- ☐ Understood
- ☐ Used in speech
- ☐ Used in writing

13. Grasp
- ☐ Understood
- ☐ Used in speech
- ☐ Used in writing

14. Hemisphere
- ☐ Understood
- ☐ Used in speech
- ☐ Used in writing

15. Hobbled
- ☐ Understood
- ☐ Used in speech
- ☐ Used in writing

16. Incidentally
- ☐ Understood
- ☐ Used in speech
- ☐ Used in writing

17. Impudent
- ☐ Understood
- ☐ Used in speech
- ☐ Used in writing

18. Inhabitant
- ☐ Understood
- ☐ Used in speech
- ☐ Used in writing

19. Insist
- ☐ Understood
- ☐ Used in speech
- ☐ Used in writing

20. Intrepid
- ☐ Understood
- ☐ Used in speech
- ☐ Used in writing

21. Liberate
- ☐ Understood
- ☐ Used in speech
- ☐ Used in writing

22. Lope
- ☐ Understood
- ☐ Used in speech
- ☐ Used in writing

23. Manicure
- ☐ Understood
- ☐ Used in speech
- ☐ Used in writing

24. Merely
- ☐ Understood
- ☐ Used in speech
- ☐ Used in writing

25. Oasis
- ☐ Understood
- ☐ Used in speech
- ☐ Used in writing

26. Opportunity
- ☐ Understood
- ☐ Used in speech
- ☐ Used in writing

27. Pallid
- ☐ Understood
- ☐ Used in speech
- ☐ Used in writing

28. Perilous
- ☐ Understood
- ☐ Used in speech
- ☐ Used in writing

29. Perpetual
- ☐ Understood
- ☐ Used in speech
- ☐ Used in writing

30. Persists
- ☐ Understood
- ☐ Used in speech
- ☐ Used in writing

31. Pharmacy
- ☐ Understood
- ☐ Used in speech
- ☐ Used in writing

32. Plead
- ☐ Understood
- ☐ Used in speech
- ☐ Used in writing

33. Pledge
- ☐ Understood
- ☐ Used in speech
- ☐ Used in writing

34. Procession
- ☐ Understood
- ☐ Used in speech
- ☐ Used in writing

35. Ramble
- ☐ Understood
- ☐ Used in speech
- ☐ Used in writing

36. Precipitation
- ☐ Understood
- ☐ Used in speech
- ☐ Used in writing

37. Referendum
- ☐ Understood
- ☐ Used in speech
- ☐ Used in writing

38. Reservoir
- ☐ Understood
- ☐ Used in speech
- ☐ Used in writing

39. Sapphire
- ☐ Understood
- ☐ Used in speech
- ☐ Used in writing

40. Scald
- ☐ Understood
- ☐ Used in speech
- ☐ Used in writing

41. Scapegoat
- ☐ Understood
- ☐ Used in speech
- ☐ Used in writing

42. Sheer
- ☐ Understood
- ☐ Used in speech
- ☐ Used in writing

43. Structure
- ☐ Understood
- ☐ Used in speech
- ☐ Used in writing

44. Tragedy
- ☐ Understood
- ☐ Used in speech
- ☐ Used in writing

45. Tropics
- ☐ Understood
- ☐ Used in speech
- ☐ Used in writing

46. Trinket
- ☐ Understood
- ☐ Used in speech
- ☐ Used in writing

47. Trespass
- ☐ Understood
- ☐ Used in speech
- ☐ Used in writing

48. Vertigo
- ☐ Understood
- ☐ Used in speech
- ☐ Used in writing

49. Tilt
- ☐ Understood
- ☐ Used in speech
- ☐ Used in writing

50. Wreath
- ☐ Understood
- ☐ Used in speech
- ☐ Used in writing

Wondrous Words

Section Eight

Walt: "Apparently, this kid is a really dedicated snooker player. He´s a ten frames a day man!"

Adopt
(uh DOPT)
to bring up a child of other parents

Ailment
an illness

Anxious
(ANG shus)
worried

Apparently
(uh PA runt li)
easily seen; obvious; seeming to be true

Burden
a load; something you have to put up with

Chalet
(SHAL ay)
a small wooden house

Counterfeit
(COWN tuh fit)
fake, imitation

Dedicated
to be fully committed to something

Demolish
(di MOL ish)
to destroy, smash down

Diabolical
(dy uh BOL icl)
dreadful, appalling

Dispatch
(dis PACH)
to send off

Eavesdrop
(EEVS drop)
to listen secretly

Evidently
clearly

Forgery
(FOR jer i)
a fake, an imitation

Furious
(FIOR i us)
extremely angry

Gratitude
(GRAT it yood)
thankfulness

Grimace
(GRIM is or grim AYS)
an ugly facial expression

Hoax
(hohcs)
a trick played on someone

Immediate
(i MEE di ut)
straight away

Incessant
(in SES unt)
non-stop

Walt: "Evidently we're in for some incessant darts action"

Winnie: "To be a bowling champ requires persistent practice."

Inquiry
(in CWY ri)
an investigation

Inundate
(IN un dayt)
to flood

Isolate
(EI suh layt)
to put away from others

Locate
(lo CAYT)
to find

Mallet
(MAL it)
a wooden hammer

Melancholy
(MEL un coly)
a depressed state of mind

Miser
(MY zuh)
a mean, stingy person

Modest
self-conscious, not showing-off; not a large amount

Persistent
(per SIST unt)
constantly repeated

Physician
(fi ZISH un)
a doctor

Prosecuted
charged with a criminal offence

Recollect
(rec uh LECT)
to remember

Relegate
to be sent to a lower position

Reluctant
(ri LUC tunt)
unwilling to take part in

Remedy
a cure

Repulsive
(ri PUL siv)
disgusting

Residence
the place where you live

Resume
(riz YOOM)
to begin again after an interruption

Rigid
stiff

Rubble
broken pieces of building material

Walt: "I´m a bit reluctant to resume playing against the chess champion."

Winnie: "I'm keeping a tally and you've won virtually every game."

Sachet
(SASH ay)
a small packet used as a container

Scoundrel
a bad, dishonest person

Shrivel
to wrinkle and dry up

Slumber
to sleep

Tally
a record of the score or number; to add up

Transparent
(trans PA runt)
see-through

Vast
enormous

Virtually
almost entirely

Wary
(WAIR i)
careful, cautious

Wrench
(rench)
to pull hard, to jerk

Crossword

Across:

4	To find
6	A mean, stingy person
9	Cautious
10	To bring up the child of other parents
11	To sleep
13	Huge
14	A copy
15	A load to carry

Down:

1	A trick
2	A cure
3	A small wooden house
5	To put away from others
7	A wooden hammer
8	To dry up
12	Stiff

Word Search

```
G A W A K D S C O U N D R E L
R F U R I O U S K A T H E N Y
A A W R H L D H T K B H C A W
T S W V I B M O D E S T O V D
I W R E N C H E C A B O N I T
T W Q T C A Q B N T T G S N R
U Q E V U Z D G B T E P U Q A
D Q W R R W F B G T A A L U N
E K I L A Y T H A T V R T I S
A W V G B W H B C Y E A W R P
V M D S L H T H Q A S M B Y A
Q I M M E D I A T E D W H K R
R A N I L O C A B O R W T O E
A N X I O U S Y T A O Q W U N
U R E S I D E N C E P B T S T
```

Games

1. Ailment
2. Anxious
3. Consult
4. Dispatch
5. Eavesdrop
6. Furious
7. Gratitude
8. Immediate
9. Incurable
10. Inquiry
11. Modest
12. Residence
13. Scoundrel
14. Transparent
15. Wrench

This page is photocopiable for classroom use only.

SECTION 8 - CHECKLIST

1. **Adopt**
   ☐ Understood
   ☐ Used in speech
   ☐ Used in writing

2. **Ailment**
   ☐ Understood
   ☐ Used in speech
   ☐ Used in writing

3. **Anxious**
   ☐ Understood
   ☐ Used in speech
   ☐ Used in writing

4. **Apparently**
   ☐ Understood
   ☐ Used in speech
   ☐ Used in writing

5. **Burden**
   ☐ Understood
   ☐ Used in speech
   ☐ Used in writing

6. **Chalet**
   ☐ Understood
   ☐ Used in speech
   ☐ Used in writing

7. **Counterfeit**
   ☐ Understood
   ☐ Used in speech
   ☐ Used in writing

8. **Dedicated**
   ☐ Understood
   ☐ Used in speech
   ☐ Used in writing

9. **Demolished**
   ☐ Understood
   ☐ Used in speech
   ☐ Used in writing

10. **Diabolical**
    ☐ Understood
    ☐ Used in speech
    ☐ Used in writing

11. **Dispatch**
    ☐ Understood
    ☐ Used in speech
    ☐ Used in writing

12. **Eavesdrop**
    ☐ Understood
    ☐ Used in speech
    ☐ Used in writing

13. **Evidently**
    ☐ Understood
    ☐ Used in speech
    ☐ Used in writing

14. **Forgery**
    ☐ Understood
    ☐ Used in speech
    ☐ Used in writing

15. **Furious**
    ☐ Understood
    ☐ Used in speech
    ☐ Used in writing

16. **Gratitude**
    ☐ Understood
    ☐ Used in speech
    ☐ Used in writing

17. **Grimace**
    ☐ Understood
    ☐ Used in speech
    ☐ Used in writing

18. **Hoax**
    ☐ Understood
    ☐ Used in speech
    ☐ Used in writing

19. **Immediate**
    ☐ Understood
    ☐ Used in speech
    ☐ Used in writing

20. **Incessant**
    ☐ Understood
    ☐ Used in speech
    ☐ Used in writing

21. **Inquiry**
    ☐ Understood
    ☐ Used in speech
    ☐ Used in writing

22. **Inundate**
    ☐ Understood
    ☐ Used in speech
    ☐ Used in writing

23. **Isolate**
    ☐ Understood
    ☐ Used in speech
    ☐ Used in writing

24. **Locate**
    ☐ Understood
    ☐ Used in speech
    ☐ Used in writing

25. **Mallet**
    ☐ Understood
    ☐ Used in speech
    ☐ Used in writing

26. **Melancholy**
    ☐ Understood
    ☐ Used in speech
    ☐ Used in writing

27. **Miser**
    ☐ Understood
    ☐ Used in speech
    ☐ Used in writing

28. **Modest**
    ☐ Understood
    ☐ Used in speech
    ☐ Used in writing

29. **Persistent**
    ☐ Understood
    ☐ Used in speech
    ☐ Used in writing

30. **Physician**
    ☐ Understood
    ☐ Used in speech
    ☐ Used in writing

31. **Prosecuted**
    ☐ Understood
    ☐ Used in speech
    ☐ Used in writing

32. **Recollect**
    ☐ Understood
    ☐ Used in speech
    ☐ Used in writing

33. **Relegate**
    ☐ Understood
    ☐ Used in speech
    ☐ Used in writing

34. **Reluctant**
    ☐ Understood
    ☐ Used in speech
    ☐ Used in writing

35. **Remedy**
    ☐ Understood
    ☐ Used in speech
    ☐ Used in writing

36. **Repulsive**
    ☐ Understood
    ☐ Used in speech
    ☐ Used in writing

37. **Residence**
    ☐ Understood
    ☐ Used in speech
    ☐ Used in writing

38. **Resume**
    ☐ Understood
    ☐ Used in speech
    ☐ Used in writing

39. **Rigid**
    ☐ Understood
    ☐ Used in speech
    ☐ Used in writing

40. **Rubble**
    ☐ Understood
    ☐ Used in speech
    ☐ Used in writing

41. **Sachet**
    ☐ Understood
    ☐ Used in speech
    ☐ Used in writing

42. **Scoundrel**
    ☐ Understood
    ☐ Used in speech
    ☐ Used in writing

43. **Shrivel**
    ☐ Understood
    ☐ Used in speech
    ☐ Used in writing

44. **Slumber**
    ☐ Understood
    ☐ Used in speech
    ☐ Used in writing

45. **Tally**
    ☐ Understood
    ☐ Used in speech
    ☐ Used in writing

46. **Transparent**
    ☐ Understood
    ☐ Used in speech
    ☐ Used in writing

47. **Vast**
    ☐ Understood
    ☐ Used in speech
    ☐ Used in writing

48. **Virtually**
    ☐ Understood
    ☐ Used in speech
    ☐ Used in writing

49. **Wary**
    ☐ Understood
    ☐ Used in speech
    ☐ Used in writing

50. **Wrench**
    ☐ Understood
    ☐ Used in speech
    ☐ Used in writing

Wondrous Words

Section Nine

"It was **baffling** the way the **corpse** of the dead pirate was so **amiable**! He said cheerfully, "Can I **assist** you?""

Accommodate
(uh COM uh dayt)
to have room for

Accompany
(uh CUM pun i)
to go with as an escort or a friend

Amiable
(AYM yu bl)
friendly

Assist
(uh SIST)
to help

Baffling
confusing

Cobbler
a person who repairs shoes

Conspicuous
(con SPIC yoo us)
easily seen and attracting attention

Corpse
a dead body

Deteriorate
(di TEER iuh ayt)
to worsen

Diversion
(dy VER zhun)
an alternative route

Drivel
(DRIV ul)
silly talk

Encounter
(en COWN tuh)
to meet; a meeting

Establish
(es TAB lish)
to set up

Export
to send goods to another country

Fascinating
(FAS in ayt ing)
attracting strongly because of interest

Fracture
to break; a broken bone

Frequently
(FREE cwunt li)
often

Gratis
free

Gripe
to complain endlessly

Hinder
to obstruct; to hold back

Walt: "That was extremely weird. I´m confused!"

Winnie: "Don´t gripe Walt! I found it fascinating, especially when the mystery is revealed at the end."

Walt: "What a marvellous experience! Hey, you look a little ghastly Winnie. Did the dragon bite you?"
Winnie: "I loathe it when you humiliate me. What an ordeal!"

Humiliate
(hioo MIL i ayt)
to make someone feel embarrassed

Import
to bring goods from another country

Indicate
to show, to point to

Inherit
(in HE rit)
to receive from an ancestor at his/her death

Invaluable
(in VAL yuh bl)
priceless

Lethargic
(luh THAR jik)
slow and lazy

Loathe
to dislike greatly; to feel disgust

Minuscule
very small

Murky
dark and gloomy

Ordeal
(or DEEL)
a severe and testing experience

Outlandish
(out LAN dish)
very unusual

Paralysed
unable to move

Plummet
to fall sharply

Ponder
to think over carefully

Prompt
on time; to push someone into action

Quiver
(CWIV uh)
a case for carrying arrows; to shake and tremble

Replica
a very close copy

Ridicule
(RID ic yool)
to make fun of

Rogue
(ROHG)
a dishonest person

Shrub
a low-growing woody plant

Winnie: "I was paralysed upside down, then I started to quiver."
Walt: "Sorry Winnie. I didn't mean to ridicule you."

Winnie: "What a torrential storm! A real topsy-turvy evening."

Squabble
(SCWO bl)
an argument; to argue

Startle
to surprise

Strive
to try hard

Throttle
to choke

Topsy-turvy
upside down

Torrential
(tuh REN shul)
very heavy rainfall

Trivial
unimportant

Universal
(yoo ni VER sul)
present everywhere

Vacancy
(VAY cun si)
an empty job position; a room available in a hotel

Yuan
(yoo ARN)
the money in China

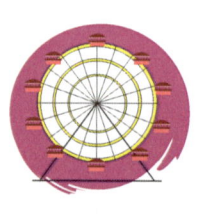

Crossword

Across:
2 Not important
5 To complain all the time
6 A broken bone
9 Free
11 To get in the way
12 The currency of China
13 Not at all clear

Down:
1 Foolish talk
3 To receive something when a family member when she or he dies
4 To send goods to another country
7 A severe test
8 To try hard
10 A large plant like a small bush

Word Search

```
C F T U N I V E R S A L W Q F
A D E T E R I O R A T E Y A A
B T Y I L E T H A R G I C A S
O V A C A N C Y K A D C O L C
F R E Q U E N T L Y O O T Y I
A S Q U A B B L E M G N A P N
T T Y J U K L O M J T S M R A
P L U M M E T O R U B P I O T
R A N I L O D A W G N I N M I
B U Y W A A S G T U H C U P N
U Y E S T A B L I S H U S T G
I T S E S R G J T N B O C S T
I N D I C A T E T G T U U H U
S H J T Y M K A K U L S L R Y
E N C O U N T E R C V N E R E
```

Miscellaneous
1. Accommodate
2. Conspicuous
3. Deteriorate
4. Encounter
5. Establish
6. Fascinating
7. Frequently
8. Indicate
9. Lethargic
10. Minuscule
11. Plummet
12. Prompt
13. Squabble
14. Universal
15. Vacancy

This page is photocopiable for classroom use only.

SECTION 9 - CHECKLIST

1. **Accommodate**
   - ☐ Understood
   - ☐ Used in speech
   - ☐ Used in writing

2. **Accompany**
   - ☐ Understood
   - ☐ Used in speech
   - ☐ Used in writing

3. **Amiable**
   - ☐ Understood
   - ☐ Used in speech
   - ☐ Used in writing

4. **Assist**
   - ☐ Understood
   - ☐ Used in speech
   - ☐ Used in writing

5. **Baffling**
   - ☐ Understood
   - ☐ Used in speech
   - ☐ Used in writing

6. **Cobbler**
   - ☐ Understood
   - ☐ Used in speech
   - ☐ Used in writing

7. **Conspicuous**
   - ☐ Understood
   - ☐ Used in speech
   - ☐ Used in writing

8. **Corpse**
   - ☐ Understood
   - ☐ Used in speech
   - ☐ Used in writing

9. **Deteriorate**
   - ☐ Understood
   - ☐ Used in speech
   - ☐ Used in writing

10. **Diversion**
    - ☐ Understood
    - ☐ Used in speech
    - ☐ Used in writing

11. **Drivel**
    - ☐ Understood
    - ☐ Used in speech
    - ☐ Used in writing

12. **Encounter**
    - ☐ Understood
    - ☐ Used in speech
    - ☐ Used in writing

13. **Establish**
    - ☐ Understood
    - ☐ Used in speech
    - ☐ Used in writing

14. **Export**
    - ☐ Understood
    - ☐ Used in speech
    - ☐ Used in writing

15. **Fascinating**
    - ☐ Understood
    - ☐ Used in speech
    - ☐ Used in writing

16. **Fracture**
    - ☐ Understood
    - ☐ Used in speech
    - ☐ Used in writing

17. **Frequently**
    - ☐ Understood
    - ☐ Used in speech
    - ☐ Used in writing

18. **Gratis**
    - ☐ Understood
    - ☐ Used in speech
    - ☐ Used in writing

19. **Gripe**
    - ☐ Understood
    - ☐ Used in speech
    - ☐ Used in writing

20. **Hinder**
    - ☐ Understood
    - ☐ Used in speech
    - ☐ Used in writing

21. **Humiliate**
    - ☐ Understood
    - ☐ Used in speech
    - ☐ Used in writing

22. **Import**
    - ☐ Understood
    - ☐ Used in speech
    - ☐ Used in writing

23. **Indicate**
    - ☐ Understood
    - ☐ Used in speech
    - ☐ Used in writing

24. **Inherit**
    - ☐ Understood
    - ☐ Used in speech
    - ☐ Used in writing

25. **Invaluable**
    - ☐ Understood
    - ☐ Used in speech
    - ☐ Used in writing

26. **Lethargic**
    - ☐ Understood
    - ☐ Used in speech
    - ☐ Used in writing

27. **Loathe**
    - ☐ Understood
    - ☐ Used in speech
    - ☐ Used in writing

28. **Minuscule**
    - ☐ Understood
    - ☐ Used in speech
    - ☐ Used in writing

29. **Murky**
    - ☐ Understood
    - ☐ Used in speech
    - ☐ Used in writing

30. **Ordeal**
    - ☐ Understood
    - ☐ Used in speech
    - ☐ Used in writing

31. **Outlandish**
    - ☐ Understood
    - ☐ Used in speech
    - ☐ Used in writing

32. **Paralysed**
    - ☐ Understood
    - ☐ Used in speech
    - ☐ Used in writing

33. **Plummet**
    - ☐ Understood
    - ☐ Used in speech
    - ☐ Used in writing

34. **Ponder**
    - ☐ Understood
    - ☐ Used in speech
    - ☐ Used in writing

35. **Prompt**
    - ☐ Understood
    - ☐ Used in speech
    - ☐ Used in writing

36. **Quiver**
    - ☐ Understood
    - ☐ Used in speech
    - ☐ Used in writing

37. **Replica**
    - ☐ Understood
    - ☐ Used in speech
    - ☐ Used in writing

38. **Ridicule**
    - ☐ Understood
    - ☐ Used in speech
    - ☐ Used in writing

39. **Rogue**
    - ☐ Understood
    - ☐ Used in speech
    - ☐ Used in writing

40. **Shrub**
    - ☐ Understood
    - ☐ Used in speech
    - ☐ Used in writing

41. **Squabble**
    - ☐ Understood
    - ☐ Used in speech
    - ☐ Used in writing

42. **Startle**
    - ☐ Understood
    - ☐ Used in speech
    - ☐ Used in writing

43. **Strive**
    - ☐ Understood
    - ☐ Used in speech
    - ☐ Used in writing

44. **Throttle**
    - ☐ Understood
    - ☐ Used in speech
    - ☐ Used in writing

45. **Topsy-turvy**
    - ☐ Understood
    - ☐ Used in speech
    - ☐ Used in writing

46. **Torrential**
    - ☐ Understood
    - ☐ Used in speech
    - ☐ Used in writing

47. **Trivial**
    - ☐ Understood
    - ☐ Used in speech
    - ☐ Used in writing

48. **Universal**
    - ☐ Understood
    - ☐ Used in speech
    - ☐ Used in writing

49. **Vacancy**
    - ☐ Understood
    - ☐ Used in speech
    - ☐ Used in writing

50. **Yuan**
    - ☐ Understood
    - ☐ Used in speech
    - ☐ Used in writing

Wondrous Words

Section Ten

Winnie: "My parents adored the music of the 70s."

Admire
(ad MYR)
to think someone or something's great

Adored
(uh DORD)
loved or respected greatly

Alternative
(ol TERN uh tiv)
a different choice

Ancestor
a family member from earlier times

Benevolent
(buh NEV uh lunt)
kind

Bewildered
(bi WIL derd)
confused

Chaos
(CAY os)
a confused, crazy situation

Colossal
(cul OS ul)
enormous

Convince
(con VINS)
to persuade; to make someone believe

Cunning
crafty

Delicate
(DEL i cut)
very finely made, easily broken; easily upset

Detached
(di TACHT)
not attached; separated

Donation
(doh NAY shun)
a gift to a charitable cause

Eerie
(EER i)
spooky

Elated
(i LAY tud)
very happy

Emotions
(i MOH shuns)
strong feelings of joy, love, hate, fear or sadness

Fiasco
(fi AS co)
a complete failure

Fictitious
(fic TISH us)
made up, false

Gargoyle
a drain spout on a building with a very ugly face

Harmonica
(har MON ic uh)
a mouth organ

Walt: "I´ve written this great fictitious story called "The Gargoyle Comes Alive"

87

LITERATURE PRIZES

Walt: "I´m hoping to get it *illustrated*. It might become a successful *novel* and make me *prosperous*!"

Homicide
the act of murder

Illustrate
(IL us tray t)
to provide pictures

Immense
(i MENS)
huge, enormous

Immerse
(im ERS)
to dip in a liquid; to be fully absorbed in your actions

Legend
(LEJ und)
the key to a map; a folk story

Limerick
a short funny poem

Literature
(LIT er it yer)
all writings but especially those considered excellent

Media
(MEE di uh)
radio, TV, newspapers and the internet

Metropolis
(muh TROP ul is)
a large city

Novel
new, unusual; a long, fictional story

Mutiny
(MIOO tin i)
a rebellion

Ogre
(OH ger)
a monster

Peculiar
(puc YOOL i uh)
unusual, strange

Prosperous
well-off

Provoked
(pruh VOHCT)
driven to anger

Quote
(CWOHT)
to repeat a phrase or passage from some writing

Resemble
(ri ZEM bl)
to look like

Reveal
(ri VEEL)
to show

Ruffian
a violent, brutal person

Sarcastic
(sar CAS tic)
a cutting remark used to hurt

Winnie: "The captain´s peculiar orders provoked the ruffians in the crew to mutiny."

"Remember, as you are about to terminate "Wondrous Words" it is vital that you do a thorough revision of the check lists at the end."

Seldom
not often, rarely

Sturdy
strongly built

Terminate
to end

Thesaurus
(thi SOR us)
a book of words, their synonyms and antonyms

Thorough
(THU ruh)
complete

Trounce
to defeat heavily

Utterly
completely, absolutely

Vital
(VY tul)
essential, alive, important

Widow
a woman whose husband has died

Widower
a man whose wife has died

Crossword

Across:
1. Not often
5. A woman whose husband has died
7. You think he's really good!
8. To show
11. Very happy
12. A family member from earlier times
13. A mad situation!

Down:
2. Radio and TV for example
3. Very important
4. A really old story
6. A monster
9. Really strong
10. A complete failure

Word Search

```
A W I N C O N V I N C E T M C
A L A P R T T O M Q T M U E O
N A T D B N O M U U U O B T L
Y Y B E N E V O L E N T W R O
T E W L R B E N E R C I I O S
R T A I I N A F Y Y G O D P S
O N Y C E T A T U B I N O O A
U O E A A L D T T O S S W L L
N U T T A D O T I Y T A E I V
C T I E O N N G N V N I R S I
E T G V R U A T U M E B H T C
M E H T T J T R E S E M B L E
A R H N I L I T E R A T U R E
R L T T J M O C H U N T I C N
K Y I M M E N S E A I M E E M
```

The Arts
1. Alternative
2. Benevolent
3. Colossal
4. Convince
5. Delicate
6. Donation
7. Emotions
8. Immense
9. Literature
10. Metropolis
11. Query
12. Resemble
13. Trounce
14. Utterly
15. Widower

This page is photocopiable for classroom use only.

SECTION 10 - CHECKLIST

1. Admire
- ☐ Understood
- ☐ Used in speech
- ☐ Used in writing

2. Adored
- ☐ Understood
- ☐ Used in speech
- ☐ Used in writing

3. Alternative
- ☐ Understood
- ☐ Used in speech
- ☐ Used in writing

4. Ancestor
- ☐ Understood
- ☐ Used in speech
- ☐ Used in writing

5. Benevolent
- ☐ Understood
- ☐ Used in speech
- ☐ Used in writing

6. Bewildered
- ☐ Understood
- ☐ Used in speech
- ☐ Used in writing

7. Chaos
- ☐ Understood
- ☐ Used in speech
- ☐ Used in writing

8. Colossal
- ☐ Understood
- ☐ Used in speech
- ☐ Used in writing

9. Convince
- ☐ Understood
- ☐ Used in speech
- ☐ Used in writing

10. Cunning
- ☐ Understood
- ☐ Used in speech
- ☐ Used in writing

11. Delicate
- ☐ Understood
- ☐ Used in speech
- ☐ Used in writing

12. Detached
- ☐ Understood
- ☐ Used in speech
- ☐ Used in writing

13. Donation
- ☐ Understood
- ☐ Used in speech
- ☐ Used in writing

14. Eerie
- ☐ Understood
- ☐ Used in speech
- ☐ Used in writing

15. Elated
- ☐ Understood
- ☐ Used in speech
- ☐ Used in writing

16. Emotions
- ☐ Understood
- ☐ Used in speech
- ☐ Used in writing

17. Fiasco
- ☐ Understood
- ☐ Used in speech
- ☐ Used in writing

18. Fictitious
- ☐ Understood
- ☐ Used in speech
- ☐ Used in writing

19. Gargoyle
- ☐ Understood
- ☐ Used in speech
- ☐ Used in writing

20. Harmonica
- ☐ Understood
- ☐ Used in speech
- ☐ Used in writing

21. Homicide
- ☐ Understood
- ☐ Used in speech
- ☐ Used in writing

22. Illustrated
- ☐ Understood
- ☐ Used in speech
- ☐ Used in writing

23. Immense
- ☐ Understood
- ☐ Used in speech
- ☐ Used in writing

24. Immerse
- ☐ Understood
- ☐ Used in speech
- ☐ Used in writing

25. Legend
- ☐ Understood
- ☐ Used in speech
- ☐ Used in writing

26. Limerick
- ☐ Understood
- ☐ Used in speech
- ☐ Used in writing

27. Literature
- ☐ Understood
- ☐ Used in speech
- ☐ Used in writing

28. Media
- ☐ Understood
- ☐ Used in speech
- ☐ Used in writing

29. Metropolis
- ☐ Understood
- ☐ Used in speech
- ☐ Used in writing

30. Mutiny
- ☐ Understood
- ☐ Used in speech
- ☐ Used in writing

31. Novel
- ☐ Understood
- ☐ Used in speech
- ☐ Used in writing

32. Ogre
- ☐ Understood
- ☐ Used in speech
- ☐ Used in writing

33. Peculiar
- ☐ Understood
- ☐ Used in speech
- ☐ Used in writing

34. Prosperous
- ☐ Understood
- ☐ Used in speech
- ☐ Used in writing

35. Provoked
- ☐ Understood
- ☐ Used in speech
- ☐ Used in writing

36. Quote
- ☐ Understood
- ☐ Used in speech
- ☐ Used in writing

37. Resemble
- ☐ Understood
- ☐ Used in speech
- ☐ Used in writing

38. Reveal
- ☐ Understood
- ☐ Used in speech
- ☐ Used in writing

39. Ruffian
- ☐ Understood
- ☐ Used in speech
- ☐ Used in writing

40. Sarcastic
- ☐ Understood
- ☐ Used in speech
- ☐ Used in writing

41. Seldom
- ☐ Understood
- ☐ Used in speech
- ☐ Used in writing

42. Sturdy
- ☐ Understood
- ☐ Used in speech
- ☐ Used in writing

43. Terminate
- ☐ Understood
- ☐ Used in speech
- ☐ Used in writing

44. Thesaurus
- ☐ Understood
- ☐ Used in speech
- ☐ Used in writing

45. Thorough
- ☐ Understood
- ☐ Used in speech
- ☐ Used in writing

46. Trounce
- ☐ Understood
- ☐ Used in speech
- ☐ Used in writing

47. Utterly
- ☐ Understood
- ☐ Used in speech
- ☐ Used in writing

48. Vital
- ☐ Understood
- ☐ Used in speech
- ☐ Used in writing

49. Widow
- ☐ Understood
- ☐ Used in speech
- ☐ Used in writing

50. Widower
- ☐ Understood
- ☐ Used in speech
- ☐ Used in writing

Answers

Section One

Crossword solution:
- 1A: AITCH
- 3A: OAF
- 5D: F...
- 6A: NOTION
- 7A: LIVID
- 8A: TASK
- 12A: WRATH
- 13A: ESSENTIAL

Wordsearch hidden words: RETORT, CASTIGATE, NICOTINE, CONDUCTOR, EXAGGERATE, EVAPORATE, LENIENT, TORRID, QUARREL, MONOTONOUS

Section Two

Crossword solution:
- 4A: BLEAK
- 5A: ARTERY
- 6A: RESIDE
- 8A: DEVOUR
- 10A: MORSEL
- 12A: VOMIT
- 13A: HESITATE

Wordsearch hidden words: LAVATORY, INDULGE, AGRICULTURE, ENCLOSE, PRECISE, TRANSLATE, KATHERINE, DISAPPROVE, GROTESQUE

Section Three

Crossword solution:
- 1A: PAUPER
- 3D: M...
- 4A: ORAL
- 7A: PAMPER
- 8A: ENVIOUS
- 9A: DETEST
- 11A: GAPE
- 12A: FABULOUS
- 13A: AFFLUENT

Wordsearch hidden words: ROUGHAGE, RESEMBLE, HIDEOUS, OBEDIENT, CONTINENTAL, SCORCH, ECCENTRIC, REMORSE, KATHERINE, ARTIFICIAL

93

Section Four

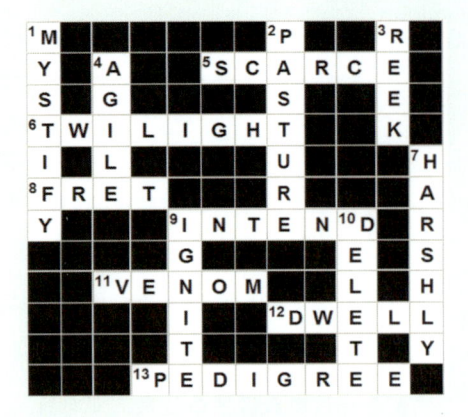

Crossword
```
 ¹M  .   .   .   ²P  .  ³R
  Y  .  ⁴A  .  ⁵S  C  A  R  C  E
  S  .   G  .   .   .   E
 ⁶T  W  I  L  I  G  H  T  .  .
  I  .   L  .   .   .   U  .  ⁷H
 ⁸F  R  E  T  .   .   R  .   A
  Y  .   .   .  ⁹I  N  T  E ¹⁰D
  .  .   G  .   .   .   .   .  E
  .  .  ¹¹V  E   N  O  M   .  L
  .  .   I  .   .  ¹²D  W  E  L  L
  .  .   T  .   .   .   .   T   .  Y
  .  .  ¹³P E  D  I  G  R  E   E
```

Word search
```
HYGENERATIONARQ
IPJKUQNPLUMAGEU
HUKAMVOPDENSINA
IRQEETUAGAIMEED
LSYARBNLANGELLR
LUNBONQLEEHUKLU
UETUUEDIALOGUEP
MMOPSBMNAQNTYML
ILCABOPGESTUREE
NAVANSEETHINGAA
ANESRANILOCABOM
TQRCRTUIMMATURE
EBMEKATHERINEAN
NKINQUNICORNABM
AZNDESCENDUIOPM
```

Section Five

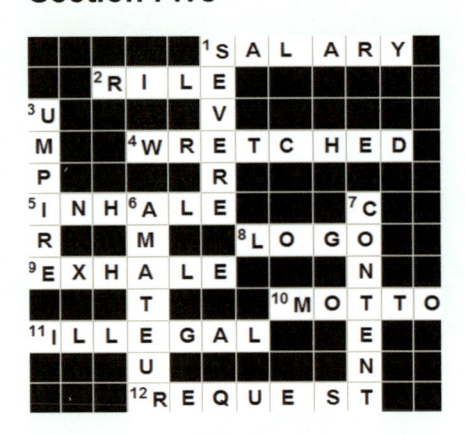

Crossword
```
              ¹S A L A R Y
      ²R I L E
 ³U   M       V
  M   .  ⁴W R E T C H E D
  P   .  R
 ⁵I N H⁶A L E       ⁷C
  R   M      ⁸L O G O
 ⁹E X H A L E
      T      ¹⁰M O T T O
     ¹¹I L L E G A L
      U              N
     ¹²R E Q U E S T
```

Word search
```
RABTMOTIVATIOND
KUAKATHERINENHE
PREBNPREVIOUSOV
RAFHAEAGYTUBIOA
ELIMINATERTTKLS
VXVBTJDAKTSAAIT
ETJKLSTOEIOHGGA
NBOPPONENTTDTAT
TEGHJKCEETHUNE
WQAQERHJLNDAWRB
AWGSENSATIONALT
GTEEFNEGOTIATEY
CIRCUMSTANCESLJ
TYIGHATEMPORARY
TPERMANENTAYEHT
```

Section Six

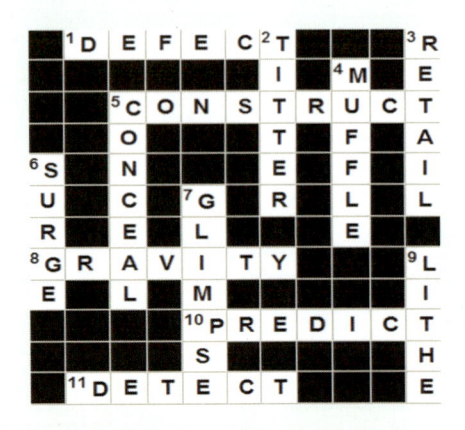

Crossword
```
    ¹D E F E C ²T         ³R
            I  .  ⁴M       E
         ⁵C O N S T R U C  T
            O     T  F     A
  ⁶S        N     E  F     I
   U        C  ⁷G  R  L    L
   R        E  L     E
  ⁸G R A V I T Y       ⁹L
   E        L  M        I
            .  .  ¹⁰P R E D I C T
            .  .   S        H
           ¹¹D E T E C T    E
```

Word search
```
FEXCURSIONAEHPA
RGHBRITTLEEHYEN
NIMBLEETUNRRTRN
TAWUTTTYCVUISE
IRRTNUHGGHNYNOD
NATJCBOFRAGMENT
ENFROISERNERFNR
VSJFNNCYKTARFEA
ILLSSTOYKIWYILN
TUOACEPUJNJECCQ
ACQUIREBHGTAIAU
BEOUOIAWTNMTEBI
LNFTUOTUNTYFNOL
ETSGSRANILOTTGM
FTDBAPEDESTRIAN
```

Section Seven

	¹M	²P	E	R	³I	L	O	U	S
⁴L		E			N				
O	R	E		⁵S	H	E	⁶E	R	
⁷P	L	E	A	D		I		V	
E		L	⁸G	R	A	S	P	E	
		Y		E		T		N	
⁹O	A	¹⁰S	I	S		¹¹C		T	
		C				E		U	
		A			¹²R	A	M	B	L	E
		L				S		L	
		¹³D	I	L	U	T	E	Y	

```
R E EVACUATE A S T L Y
SAPPHIRE J P I Y L I B
A V S Q T M R I GHASTLY
HEMISPHERE F I L P P
U R T T W U DAVID D I H E
R T I DADS R T Y I ANAR
E I T E M E ABOLISH R P
V G T L Y N A KOMI TAME
R O T I I T Y T I Y U ABAT
R I DG JOCELYN R I C U
ADHESIVE E R A D T Y A
I B ANTYYUUMT L A U L
B L L T R Q R T K L L Y N P Y
OPPORTUNITY K T U P
N U T U EMIGRATE T I O
```

Section Eight

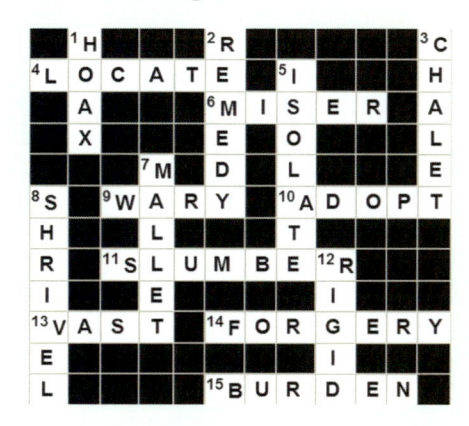

	¹H			²R				³C
⁴L	O	C	A	T	E		⁵I		H
	A				⁶M	I	S	E	R
	X				E		O		A
			⁷M		D		L		L
⁸S		⁹W	A	R	Y		¹⁰A	D	O	P	T
H			L			T			
R		¹¹S	L	U	M	B	E	¹²R	
I			E					I	
¹³V	A	S	T		¹⁴F	O	R	G	E	R	Y
E								I	
L					¹⁵B	U	R	D	E	N

```
GAWAKD SCOUNDREL
R FURIOUS KATHENY
A AWRH L DHTKBH C AW
T SWV I B MODESTO V D
I WRENCHE CABO N I T
T WQT CAQBN T T G S N R
U QEV UZDGB TEPUQA
D QWR R WFBGT A A L UN
E K I L AYTHAT V R T I S
A WVG B WHB C YEAWR P
V MDS L HT H QASMB Y A
Q IMMEDIATED WH K R
RAN I LOCABOR WTOE
ANXIOUS YTAOQWUN
U RESIDENCE P B T S T
```

Section Nine

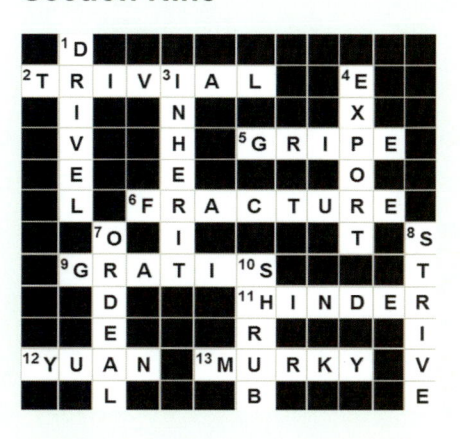

	¹D							
²T	R	I	V	³I	A	L		⁴E
	I			N				X
	V			H		⁵G	R	I	P	E
	E			E				O
	L		⁶F	R	A	C	T	U	R	E
		⁷O		I				T		⁸S
		⁹G	R	A	T	I	¹⁰S			T
		D					¹¹H	I	N	D	E	R
		E					E			I
¹²Y	U	A	N		¹³M	U	R	K	Y		V
		L				B				E

```
C F T UNIVERSAL WQ F
A DETERIORATE Y A A
B T Y I LETHARGIC A S
O VACANCY KAD COL C
FREQUENTLY OO T Y I
A SQUABBLE M GNAPN
T T Y JUKLO M J T SMRA
PLUMMETO RUB P I OT
R ANILO DAWG N INM I
BUYWA ASGTUH C UPN
UY ESTABLISH USTG
I T S ESRGJTNBO CS T
INDICATE TGTUU HU
S H J TYMKAKUL S L RY
ENCOUNTER C VN ERE
```

95

Section Ten

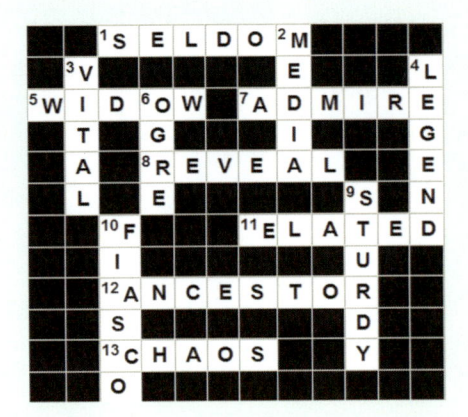

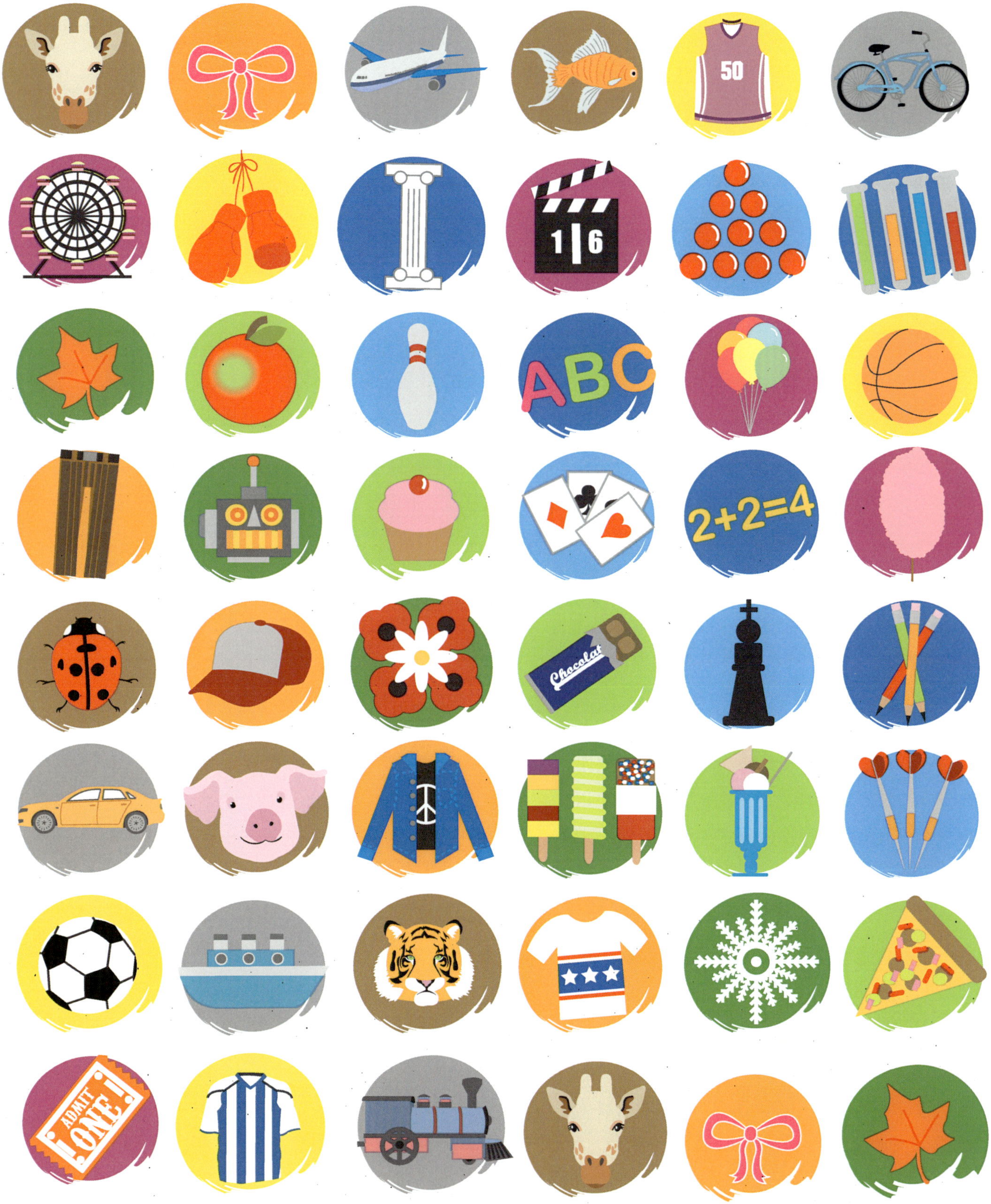
50
1 6
ABC
2+2=4
Chocolat
ADMIT ONE!

Lightning Source UK Ltd.
Milton Keynes UK
UKRC02n1544240217
295233UK00004B/35